SPRINTER SACRE

SPRINTER SACRE

THE IMPOSSIBLE DREAM

EDITED BY

BROUGH SCOTT

RACING POST

First published in Great Britain in 2016 by
Racing Post Books
27 Kingfisher Court, Hambridge Road, Newbury, Berkshire, RG14 5SJ

10 9 8 7 6 5 4 3 2 1

A catalogue record for this book is available from the British Library.

ISBN 978-1-910498-91-0

Cover designed by Jay Vincent
Text designed by J Schwartz & Co.
Printed and bound in the Czech Republic by Finidr

www.racingpost.com/shop

Photographic Acknowledgements
All the photos are copyright © Racing Post except the following:
Christophe Masle: page 12
Cranhamphotos: page 123
Fiona Crick: pages 13, 24, 70, 119, 130, 131, 160
Getty Images: pages 9, 10–11, 49, 71, 72–73, 86, 89, 91, 109, 110, 112, 137, 140, 150, 163, 164–165, 178
Martin Lynch: page 18
Racingfotos.com: Front Cover, pages 14, 15, 16

CONTENTS

FOREWORD
NICKY HENDERSON

AS BARRY Hills has said, this training game is all about hours of agony and moments of glory and this probably sums up the story of Sprinter Sacre. The golden years of being unbeaten and probably unbeatable over fences were followed by two years of real agony, but then the glory days came back and, as Channel 4 so wonderfully described it, the 'impossible dream' came true.

When he first arrived here he already had a look about him, a fine physique and that wonderful head. He was all quality and a great colour and mover. This does not guarantee success, let alone greatness, but he was a useful young hurdler who was good enough to be third in the Supreme Novices Hurdle when ridden for the only time by one Sir Anthony McCoy.

Once he began his chasing career it was obvious that he was very special. He had become very strong and Barry Geraghty's only concern was curbing his enthusiasm. On his third start at Newbury, having gone into a fence five lengths down on take-off, he landed three in front and was nicknamed the 'black aeroplane'. We had two seasons that saw him become the second highest rated steeplechaser of all time.

Then the agonies began and the day when Barry had to pull him up at Kempton with a heart problem plummeted us all down to earth. He had become such a public horse and a very, very proud one, but we now faced what turned out to be nearly two years in a brutal wilderness and, of course, there were days when we feared it would not happen again. Good horses never give up and the team wasn't for it either. Caroline (Mould) never put us under any pressure and every single cog in the Seven Barrows wheel did their part and somehow, if very slowly, that wheel started to go round again and the dream was alive and eventually, incredibly, in March it came true.

It was one of the great comebacks in equine folklore and a day we will never forget.

INTRODUCTION
BROUGH SCOTT

GREAT HORSES like great events need their story told. Usually it is with the wisdom of hindsight and however well done there is always a touch of reheating the potatoes. The other way is to take the chronicles of the time. Because we at the *Racing Post* are the daily chroniclers of the game, we have the chance (or the duty?), to assemble the offerings as they come. That is what we did with previous books on Sea The Stars, Kauto Star and Frankel. Sprinter Sacre is rightly amongst their number.

It helps that in Nicky Henderson the horse has a trainer who is as helpful as he is distinguished and that Caroline Mould embraced the project from the outset. Three years ago we published *Henderson's Heroes* as a record of Nicky's 'Annus Mirabilis' in which Sprinter Sacre was one of the shining stars. But while it would have been possible to imagine him one day meriting a whole volume on his own, no one back then could have dreamt of the rollercoaster ride that his own story would eventually contain.

But it is precisely because of those trials, tribulations and eventual resurrection that Sprinter Sacre has become the best loved horse in the Anglo-Irish firmament. All those awed by his brilliance in the years of zenith were shattered by the heart problem that struck him down at Kempton and so have doubly welcomed the moments this past season when the clouds rolled away and something very close to the old Sprinter Sacre ruled the roost once more.

This book is also a tribute to all those at the *Racing Post* who daily labour in our part of the sporting vineyard and it has been put together thanks to the designer skills of John Schwartz and his team at Soapbox, to the diligent enthusiasm of James Norris back at Racing Post Books and to the unfailing support of everyone close

to the horse. It was in April 1986 that a throwaway line of mine to Sheikh Mohammed 14 months earlier eventually landed us with the first edition of the *Racing Post*. The operation has given me many pleasures down the years and working on this book has been one of the sweetest. That's what a great horse can do.

AT THE RACES
6

1
PROMISE

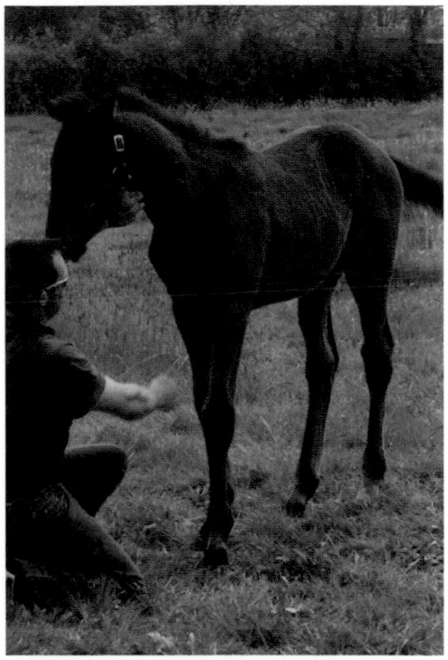

PREVIOUS SPREAD: Sprinter Sacre saunters home in the Tingle Creek 2012

ABOVE: Sprinter Sacre as a foal in Cercy-La-Tour

OPPOSITE PAGE: Sprinter Sacre gleams in the Berkshire sun as he struts his stuff on Seven Barrows' gallops

SEVEN BARROWS, the training stable takes its name from the burial ground on the downs above Lambourn that date back 4,000 years to the Bronze Age. Nicky Henderson has only been here since 1992 and every year the success that is already in legend is reinforced by a bunch of young hopefuls coming in to swell the stable strength just like talented kids into a Premier League football academy.

On 5 November 2009, one of these was a big, raw, almost black three-year-old from Juliet and David Minton's stud in Shropshire and further education with Phil and Mel Rowley close by. Sprinter Sacre was already named when he had originally come to the Mintons as part of a 20 strong 'job lot' bought by David in Burgundy 18 months earlier on behalf of Raymond Mould.

By the time Sprinter Sacre reached Seven Barrows, Caroline Mould had taken over ownership. The horse was given to Sarwar Mohammed to look after and as he got into faster work aspirant jockey Nico de Boinville furthered the education.

By the time of his first race at Ascot in February 2010 he had shown talent enough to start odds-on favourite in the 14 runner NH Flat Race that closed the card. He duly won, the fourth victory on the day for Henderson and jockey Barry Geraghty. *Racing Post's* Lambourn correspondent Rodney Masters became the first reporter to pen some words about Sprinter Sacre. None of us realised quite how many thousands were to follow.

It was Henderson and Geraghty for a four-timer when widely fanfared newcomer Sprinter Sacre justified his reputation in the bumper, though it was a close call with the more experienced King Of The Night.

'He's a lovely prospect but is a big baby and we've no plans at this stage of his career,' said Henderson.

RACING POST ANALYSIS: No more than a fair bumper, but the front two pulled away close home, with the third, in turn, clear of the remainder. The highly-regarded Sprinter Sacre overcame his lack of experience to narrowly edge out the penalised runner-up, who easily emerges as the best horse at the weights.

ASCOT
Gardiner & Theobald Standard
Open National Hunt Flat Race

AYR
Ashleybank Investments Standard
Open National Hunt Flat Race

2009-10 | 2010-11 | 2011-12 | 2012-13

FEB | MAR | APR | NOV | DEC | JAN | FEB | MAR | APR | NOV | DEC | JAN | FEB | MAR | APR | NOV | DEC | JAN | FEB | MAR | APR

Representing a yard responsiblc for two of the last four winners of this race, he was always travelling kindly under Barry Geraghty, despite briefly being interfered with, and battled well to maintain a narrow advantage when strongly challenged inside the final furlong. He is the brighter long-term prospect of the front pair, and it will be interesting to see whether he is up to defying a penalty, as many find it too big an ask.

It was two months before he ran again. Another NH Flat Race, this time at the end of the Scottish Grand National card in which Merigo had become the first Scottish-trained winner of the big race since 1982. Sprinter Sacre started 13/8 favourite and Barry Geraghty's biggest problem was pulling him up after the winning post.

RACING POST ANALYSIS: Sprinter Sacre, ridden with supreme confidence, looked the winner from a long way out and Geraghty was able to wait for his moment to pounce. A narrow winner at Ascot on his debut, the four-year-old is a nice recruit and potentially an exciting one when he switches to hurdles.

> He is a lovely prospect but is a big baby and we've no plans at this stage of his career.
>
> **NICKY HENDERSON**

King Of The Night (nearside) battles bravely but Sprinter Sacre scores a winning racecourse debut at Ascot in February 2010

Summer breaks are always important for young Henderson stars and from May until August Sprinter Sacre returned to his second home with the Mintons in Shropshire. When he came back he showed enough in his preparation over hurdles to start hot favourite on his reappearance at Ascot. He was only second that day but the RP Analysis was impressed enough to say he 'should make a fine chaser' and when he slaughtered seven rivals at Ffos Las when next seen three months later, its eulogy explained that things were likely to get even better.

Nicky Henderson could not have been more pleased with the victory of the good-looking Sprinter Sacre as the Barry Geraghty-partnered five-year-old could hardly have been more impressive in scooting away from Sorcillera.

The Seven Barrows trainer said: 'He's a very nice horse who we've always held in some regard, but he'll not have learnt

ASCOT
Redstone 'National Hunt' Novices' Hurdle

FFOS LAS
Williamhill.com Novices' Hurdle

2009-10 | 2010-11 | 2011-12 | 2012-13

FEB | MAR | APR | NOV | DEC | JAN | FEB | MAR | APR | NOV | DEC | JAN | FEB | MAR | APR | NOV | DEC | JAN | FEB | MAR | APR

much from that as they didn't go fast enough for him in the early stages.

'He was not quite right, like a few of ours at the time, when beaten at Ascot in November but he has pleased us recently and I would like to think he will be one of the team going to Cheltenham for the Stan James Supreme Novices' Hurdle.'

Sprinter Sacre was cut to 12-1 (from 25) by William Hill for the Festival contest. *(Andrew King)*

Sprinter Sacre jumps the last on route to a comfortable success at Ffos Las

RACING POST ANALYSIS: An interesting race on paper, in what looked testing conditions, but the market fully expected Sprinter Sacre, who showed plenty of ability on his hurdling debut at Ascot (2m3f), to win, and he never looked like letting his supporters down. A horse with a high cruising speed, who reportedly returned with a very dirty nose after his run at the Berkshire course, he surely has plenty more improvement to come and seems sure to develop into a Grade 1 performer. The Supreme Novices' Hurdle at Cheltenham next month is the target, but connections didn't seem fully committal afterwards, so punters may want to hold their bets for a while.

Nicky Henderson said, 'at Ascot, to the public he disappointed a little but in reality he scoped very badly after that. We were mortified but there was a reason.'

A fortnight later at Ascot he was even more impressive as the last leg of yet another four-timer for Henderson and Geraghty.

Henderson and Geraghty completed a short-priced four-timer when Sprinter Sacre cruised to an easy win in the 2m novice hurdle and Mono Man battled home a game winner of the bumper.

Sprinter Sacre is now a top-priced 10-1 chance for the Stan James Supreme Novices' in which Henderson also has second favourite Spirit Son. The trainer said: 'I'd love to put him away for chasing, but I'll have difficulty persuading Mr and

An awesome foursome approach the last as one in the 2011 Supreme Novices' Hurdle. From left to right: Al Ferof, Spirit Son, Sprinter Sacre and Cue Card

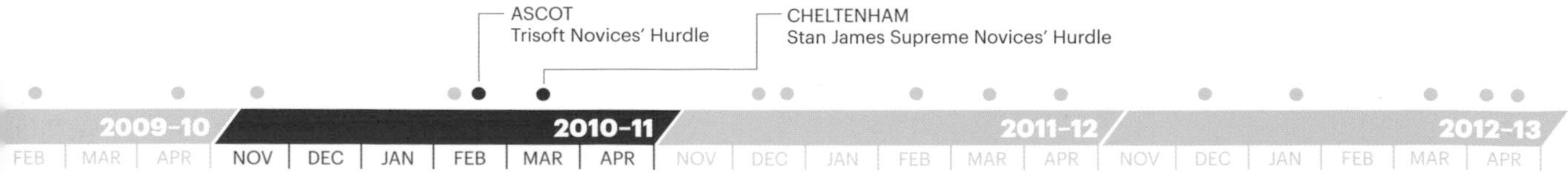

Mrs Mould, his owners, and I expect he'll go to Cheltenham. He's got serious ability and Barry is mad about him.' *(Jon Lees)*

But at Cheltenham Barry Geraghty was spoilt for Henderson choice in what was to prove one of the best Supreme Novices' ever run and finally opted for the talented Spirit Son leaving no less than AP McCoy to substitute on Sprinter Sacre. It would be the only time in his life that Sprinter Sacre started bigger than 10-1 and arguably the substitute jockey went a bit too soon.

Nicky Henderson has a poor record in this event, but it's been another cracking season so far and he held a very strong hand this year with three smart and unexposed novices. It looked turning for home as though he would have the winner as Sprinter Sacre cruised into the home straight, but he was feeling the pinch prior to hitting the last and it was his first string, Spirit Son, who rallied to take the lead there. This ex-French 5-y-o hung right to the stands' rail on the run-in, though, and looked to be feeling the quicker ground. He couldn't cope with the winner when it mattered, but ran a blinder in defeat and is a classy prospect for novice chasing. A return to easier ground should suit ideally.

Sprinter Sacre bravely held on to third and this handsome, strong-travelling performer is another that is really something to look forward to for chasing. Indeed he could well turn out the best of these over fences next season. *(David Orton)*

Sprinter's promise was all the greater because McCoy had reported that his breathing had not been perfect towards the end of the race, a problem corrected by Geoff Lane performing his standard 'hobday' operation once the horse had returned to basic fitness after his summer break. His fate seemed set fair, not so for Spirit Son who had followed Cheltenham by winning brilliantly at Aintree, only to never run again once struck down by injury.

For Sprinter Sacre and those who rode him, there was the growing delight of teaching him to jump the fences his frame and

> I'd love to put him away for chasing, but I'll have difficulty persuading Mr and Mrs Mould, his owners, and I expect he'll go to Cheltenham. He's got serious ability and Barry is mad about him.
>
> **NICKY HENDERSON**

With David Bass in the saddle, Sprinter Sacre shows his to become trademark accuracy over a fence

athleticism were begging for. The lessons went so well that he was a 2-9 favourite when eventually making his debut over the bigger fences at Doncaster. Nico de Boinville had yet to ride a single winner over jumps, so with Barry Geraghty doing stable duty at Cheltenham the mount on Sprinter Sacre was entrusted to the more experienced David Bass, one of the few jockeys who can boast a father as a music teacher and a mother as a vicar.

Divine assistance was not needed.

Supreme Novices' Hurdle third Sprinter Sacre was the star on show at Doncaster yesterday as he jumped with zest and enthusiasm on his first start over fences to win the novice chase by a comfortable 24 lengths. In the process he was cut to 6-1 from 8-1 for the Arkle with Victor Chandler.

The Nicky Henderson-trained five-year-old particularly impressed with spectacular leaps when driven into the fourth-last and the last by David Bass, who said: 'He's schooled brilliantly at home. He's by far the best horse I've sat on and he's always been the sort who would improve for a fence. He was fresh and gassy, which he was on occasions last year, and in a top-class race he should be even better.'

DONCASTER
Atteys Solicitors Novices' Chase

KEMPTON
Wayward Lad Novices' Chase

2009-10 | 2010-11 | 2011-12 | 2012-13

FEB | MAR | APR | NOV | DEC | JAN | FEB | MAR | APR | NOV | DEC | JAN | FEB | MAR | APR | NOV | DEC | JAN | FEB | MAR | APR

Henderson's assistant Ben Pauling was there to unsaddle Caroline Mould's gelding and said: 'To see him go out and jump like that is a big relief. His only slight mistake came at the water and that's because it was too small for him. He was made for a fence and he's jumped fantastically.' *(Ben Hutton)*

Nicky Henderson had been at Cheltenham.

By then we knew. I was at Cheltenham and I got a bollocking from the stewards for having my horses late to the start at Cheltenham because I was watching Sprinter's first chase at Doncaster. I reminded the steward the other day and said, 'I could not tell you at the time but I knew I had the best young chaser in years and I wanted to watch it.'

Fourteen days later he was already being touted as an Arkle challenger but not as much as Peddlers Cross, runner-up to Hurricane Fly in the previous season's Champion Hurdle, three races after Sprinter got beaten in the Supreme, and an easy winner of his first two chases. Peddlers Cross started favourite but the result was never in doubt.

SPRINTER SLAYS PEDDLERS

The clash occurred three months earlier than intended but Sprinter Sacre looked so impressive in beating Peddlers Cross at Kempton yesterday that there is now less chance of a rematch between the pair at Cheltenham next March.

The two unbeaten novices were first and second favourite for the Racing Post Arkle Trophy going into yesterday's three-runner williamhill.com Novices' Chase (registered as the Wayward Lad Novices' Chase) but while Sprinter

Sprinter Sacre at Kempton clears the last with precision as he destroys Peddlers Cross in the Wayward Lad Novices' Chase

> He is keen but that is because he is so good and powerful but he has not run away. He has settled into the last and I hope I have the same problem next month!
>
> **BARRY GERAGHTY**

Nico de Boinville enjoys his time in the saddle as Sprinter Sacre's daily companion while the pair survey their plush surroundings at Seven Barrows

exuberance and panache that Sprinter Sacre produced and none ran faster.

Despite Geraghty sitting motionless up the home straight before easing off into the last, Sprinter Sacre lowered the course record set by Barnbrook Again 22 years ago by nearly half a second.

No wonder Henderson, who had a 1-2 with last year's winner French Opera an outclassed second, was moved to say: 'He is something else. It's a bit scary really.'

Henderson, bidding to become the winning-most trainer at the Cheltenham Festival this year, had hoped Sprinter Sacre would be taught a lesson by his elders for some of the race, but was forced to concede his 'black aeroplane' left them all taxiing on the runway by halfway with the pilot not even having to reach for the thruster control. 'I feel sorry for French Opera as he was doing a good job in front,' added Henderson. 'Then this black aeroplane comes alongside and that is that!

NEWBURY
Game Spirit Chase

CHELTENHAM
Racing Post Arkle Challenge Trophy Chase

2009-10: FEB | MAR | APR
2010-11: NOV | DEC | JAN | FEB | MAR | APR
2011-12: NOV | DEC | JAN | FEB | MAR | APR
2012-13: NOV | DEC | JAN | FEB | MAR | APR

'All we were trying to do was stop him doing what he has done before – pull Barry's arms out.'

Geraghty was charitable in adding: 'He is keen but that is because he is so good and powerful, and he has not run away. He settled going into the last and I hope I have that problem next month!' Looking to the Festival, Henderson is not worried about a repetition of the Supreme Novices' last year when Sprinter Sacre looked all over the winner before weakening up the hill into third behind Al Ferof, who is in his shadow in the Arkle betting.

He said: 'He is bigger and stronger and fences were always going to bring out the best in him. He was the chaser out of all of them and we were just playing around over hurdles.'

After yesterday it looks like the chasing game could be his playground for years to come.

Despite all this, the challenge of the Arkle Chase at the Cheltenham Festival still looked a mighty one. Maybe, but Nicky Henderson was buzzing with belief.

I never usually pay much attention to race times, but his three runs over fences have been quite extraordinary even though he has never been pressed. Sprinter Sacre sauntered round at Kempton, as he'd done at Doncaster and then at Newbury. Barry was easing up from two out at Newbury, yet they broke the course record and he must have clocked some exceptional fractions. He can gain three lengths at every fence. He's the one we have that everyone is frightened of. After the Supreme last season A.P. said he was suspicious of his wind and therefore we had that rectified. Some have said he's a flat-track horse who won't come up the hill and Joe Tizzard [rider of Cue Card] says he's going to go too fast for us. We'll just do our own thing.

All roads led to the Arkle. Some cited the previous year's Cheltenham defeat to wonder if he would truly stay up the hill but Paddy

An Arkle demolition, as Barry Geraghty sits motionless aboard an imperious Sprinter Sacre crossing Cheltenham's finish line, the likes of Cue Card, Menorah and Al Ferof are left trailing in his wake

Power offered money back if he didn't win. As it happened he would have won pulling a cart.

SPRINTER FLIES IN TO CONFIRM SUPERSTAR STATUS

It was simplicity itself, a tour de force executed with ruthlessness, nonchalance and disdain. For all that it had been widely billed, it was still breathtaking to see it realised. To pay it the greatest possible compliment, it was a performance worthy of a race named after the greatest of all chasers.

Sprinter Sacre will never come close to emulating Arkle, first and foremost because he will not follow the path trod by Himself. There will be no Gold Cups, King Georges or Hennessys. The horse we marvelled at yesterday is a bubbling volcano of speed, one who possesses just enough stamina to see out a two-mile test.

Barry Geraghty celebrates as Sprinter Sacre is led into the winner's enclosure at Cheltenham after the 2012 Arkle Challenge Trophy Chase. The Henderson family are in raptures behind

Sprinter Sacre is not Arkle. He is Sprinter Sacre. That is enough. The critics will say that only five horses took him on in this Grade 1 event sponsored for the first time by the *Racing Post*, making for the Arkle's smallest ever field. There was, though, a reason for that.

Only five horses opposed Sprinter Sacre because the rest had been frightened into hiding.

They were right to be scared, for in cruising to a seven-length defeat of Cue Card, with 22 lengths back to Menorah in third, the long and scopey six-year-old confirmed himself to be an adolescent of rare and freakish ability.

'I'm speechless,' said Barry Geraghty after providing the minimal help that was needed to give boss Nicky Henderson a record-equalling 40th Cheltenham Festival success. None that

Henderson, nor the former sole record holder Fulke Walwyn, had previously enjoyed could have been achieved more impressively. Having settled better than in his previous three chase starts, Sprinter Sacre jumped to the front over the final ditch, the extravagance of his leap magnified by the mistake made by Al Ferof, who finished fourth.

Turning down the hill the race was already in safekeeping. Another soaring jump at the third last kept it safe and thereafter Geraghty enjoyed the luxury of long looks back in the

Sarwar Mohammed looks wistfully into the eyes of his extraordinary charge, Sprinter Sacre, as the new Arkle winner poses for crowds and cameras

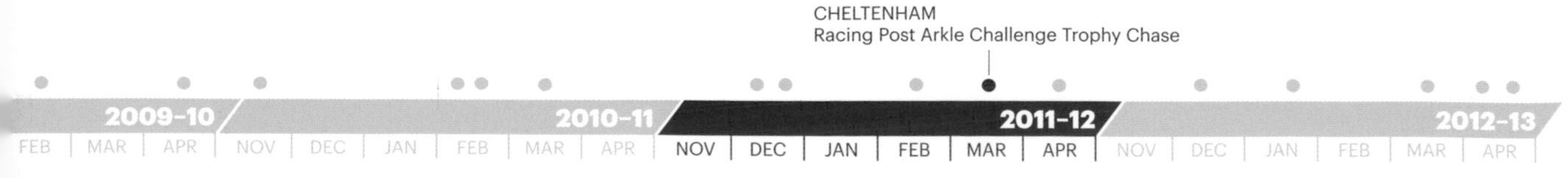

direction of vastly inferior, but still extremely talented, opponents. This was the definition of easy.

'I'm not sure I've ever ridden a horse who goes at it the way he does,' said Geraghty. 'There was plenty left. He pulled up a little in front but then I gave him a squeeze and off he went. I've never had so much pleasure from schooling a horse in my life. I was calling him Mourinho when we came in. He really is the special one.'

The special one is just 6-4 with William Hill to claim next year's Sportingbet Queen Mother Champion Chase, the contest that is sure to be his 2013 target.

Geraghty suggested that trying to stretch him over further 'would be like running Frankel in the Gold Cup'.

Henderson agreed. 'I can't see any way that he is going to need or want to go any further,' said the trainer, who eulogised about his new champion. 'He is as good an Arkle horse as we've seen for a bit,' he said. 'He looks like a proper horse and seems to do it like one.

'He has that sort of presence about him that says, "Look at me!"

'We called him the long dark aeroplane beforehand and didn't he fly! Some of what he does is ridiculous but, as I have always said, he is a dreadful show-off. He wants everyone to watch him being flash – and boy, is it worth watching.'

Joe Tizzard watched from a distance on Cue Card but described himself as 'over the moon' with the Aintree-bound runner-up. Also pleased with third home Menorah was trainer Philip Hobbs, who said: 'I'm very happy with our horse but the winner is exceptional.'

That exceptional winner is owned by Caroline Mould, who received her trophy from TV presenter Dermot O'Leary. Suitably impressed, he described Sprinter Sacre as 'a beautiful, almost arrogant-looking horse' and described what he had just witnessed as 'stunning'.

O'Leary, like all at Cheltenham, was privileged to watch a horse with the X-factor. *(Lee Mottershead)*

“

Going off too quick was the only way Sprinter Sacre was going to get beaten so the main thing was to keep him relaxed. He settled better today and he wasn't as extravagant early, which meant I could keep him back and not get competitive. I had an easier time today than I did at Newbury. He coasted in really.

BARRY GERAGHTY

He is as good an Arkle horse as we've seen for a bit. I can't see any way that he is going to need or want to go any further. If you did you would only be curtailing what he does so brilliantly.

NICKY HENDERSON

The eyes of a monster, Sprinter Sacre

By now we realised that we had what the headline would call 'A Monster' in our midst. We needed to know a lot more about him and his background. Before he ran again at Aintree, Lee Mottershead, our then Racing Journalist of The Year, went down to Seven Barrows to find out.

MONSTER OF A HORSE

When it comes to matters of romance, thoroughbred stallions tend to be males of the love 'em and leave 'em variety. Without any prior need for courtship they find themselves presented with an alluring lady, they act on their carnal instinct and then walk away, another notch added to their bedpost. Not for a second do the consequences of their actions concern them. Given the story of Sprinter Sacre, that's just as well.

Were stallions in the least bit bothered about the products of their promiscuity the Sprinter Sacre saga could have turned

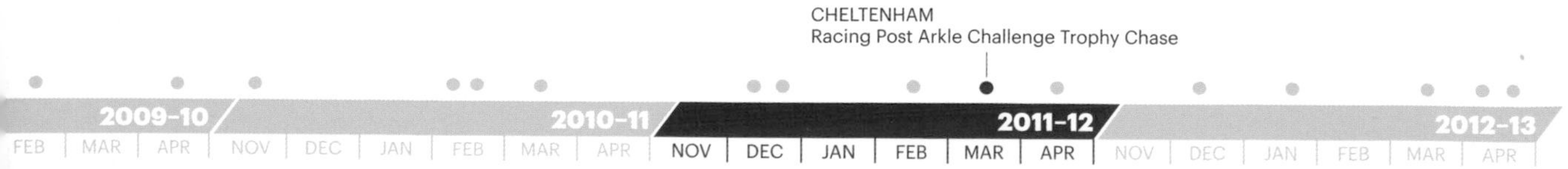

into a grubby mess, ideal fodder for a four-legged version of *The Jeremy Kyle Show*. Sitting on two seats, wide apart for safety reasons, would have been a stallion called Network and another called Dark Moondancer. In between the two, looking sheepish and shamed, would have sat a mare named Fatima III. Waiting in the wings, a camera focused on his cherubic features, would have been poor little Sprinter Sacre, just a few months old, his plight guaranteed to stimulate sounds of sympathy from the audience. Those at the centre of the drama and those watching it being played out would have been united in their desire to know the answer to one question: who's the father?

Now we know the answer. We also know that Sprinter Sacre, imperious winner of the Racing Post Arkle and now bound for Aintree, is high on the list of the most exceptional novice chasers of the modern era. Yet the story that took him to superstardom has been far from simple. Jumping's new top-of-the-bill performer is a horse who was once ignored by his present connections and subsequently acquired as part of a job lot deal.

Should his abundant promise be fulfilled, he could soon enough earn comparison with the finest two-mile chasers of all time. That, though, is his future. His past began in central France where a young sheep and cattle farmer decided that, like so many of his neighbours, he wanted to breed a racehorse.

Cercy-La-Tour, in the Burgundy region of the Nièvre, is famous in French racing as the home of the AQPS (Autre Que Pur Sang) jumper. The tough, hardy animals, whose blood is a mixture of thoroughbred and non-thoroughbred, have a rich tradition in France, principally thanks to the exploits of Auteuil legend Al Capone II, a seven-time winner of the track's King George VI Chase equivalent race, the Prix la Haye Jousselin. Al Capone was bred in Cercy by Jacques Cypres, who also masterminded the mating that resulted in Cheltenham Gold Cup hero The Fellow. Two decades on from that conception, the Cypres family were responsible for the mare who brought us Sprinter Sacre.

Sprinter Sacre at the head of Nicky Henderson's increasingly star-studded string

Fatima was bred and owned by Jacques Cypres's father Bernard, who gave the mare to an elderly gentleman. The beneficiary of Bernard's kindness then decided to profit from the gift and sold the mare, albeit for not much, to another Cercy resident Christophe Masle, coincidentally a friend of the Cypres family. Masle, more accustomed to working with his 80 cows than his one broodmare, wanted to breed from Fatima and, keen to keep things local, opted to do business with the town's Haras National de Cercy-La-Tour. The problem facing Masle was that the stud had two suitable stallions, Network and Dark Moondancer. Choosing between them caused Masle no end of trouble.

Jacques Cypres's wife Andrée says: 'Christophe is a small man with a small voice. He was completely inexperienced at breeding racehorses and what has happened is just a fairytale for him.

'He had been planning to send Fatima to Dark Moondancer but when he got to the stud he changed his mind and went for Network instead. Network covered the mare but she then came in season again so it was assumed that she was barren. Christophe therefore decided it would be best to have her covered by Dark Moondancer and, this time, Fatima was found to be pregnant.

'She gave birth to Sprinter Sacre in April 2006 and in the August of that year Christophe entered them both in the combined mother and foal class at the Decizes AQPS Show that we have been organising for many years. The foal was listed as being by Dark Moondancer and that is what I had printed in the programme but then we got a letter from the stud to say the foal's blood matched not Dark Moondancer's but Network's.

'We realised Network had succeeded in getting Fatima in foal. It transpired that his semen lasted very long. And that's the beginning of the Sprinter Sacre story. Voilà!'

The story, however, was to take many more twists. The Decizes sale, held within earshot of the Loire's rippling waters, has further cemented the Cypres family's place in the French bloodstock industry. The likes of Sir Des Champs and Rubi Light had previously both appeared in one of their event's show classes, but in 2006 the bar was raised even higher.

Aside from Sprinter Sacre, future four-time Cheltenham Festival winner Quevega was also competing, both horses coming under the glare of two visiting Brits, trainer Nicky Henderson and bloodstock agent David Minton. One man would end up arranging the purchase of Sprinter Sacre, the other would become his trainer. That, though, was still some way off. Indeed, neither Henderson nor Minton have any recollection of their first encounter with a horse who would soon become an important part of their lives.

'We did buy a horse that day but I don't remember seeing Sprinter Sacre,' admits Henderson. 'All I know is that he and Quevega were there at the same show on the same day. Both were also there to be sold, so I suppose we missed the opportunity.'

The opportunity was to come knocking 17 months down the line. The first man to take it was leading French jumps owner Robert Fougedoire, who paid just €6,000 to acquire the foal who topped his Decizes class. In January 2008, Fougedoire gave Minton a chance to make amends for an earlier oversight. 'I have to say I can't remember the slightest thing about Sprinter Sacre from that day in Decizes,' says Minton, who was having breakfast with owner Raymond Mould on the morning of Cheltenham's Festival Trials Day when informed that Fougedoire was keen to do business.

'Our French agent David Powell informed us that Mr Fougedoire was ill and wanted to sell all his young stock, which comprised of three-year-olds, two-year-olds and yearlings. The price for all 22 horses was €300,000. Raymond fancied having a go at that, so the following Tuesday the vet Buffy Shirley-Beavan and myself went across on the ferry from Portsmouth to Caen and then drove three-quarters of an hour to Haras de Hoguenet, where all the horses were based. None of them stood out but they were a very good-looking bunch as a whole. There was only one we didn't want, so the deal was done.' Mould, however, had wanted the deal to yield further transactions. His plan had been to keep a handful of the horses and sell the rest. Unfortunately for Mould, the credit crash intervened. 'We couldn't sell a store horse for love nor money,' recalls Mould, while Minton vividly remembers his long-standing client's reaction. 'He said: 'Sod it, let's race them.''

Sodding it and racing them proved to be one of the best decisions Mould has ever made. Among the batch of 21 were not only Sprinter Sacre but this season's Cheltenham Grade 2 winner Batonnier, the classy Tour Des Champs, John Smith's Grand National candidate Viking Blond and Astracad, who in December won the Cheltenham handicap chase named in memory of Mould's late wife Jenny.

Carrying the colours of Mould's second wife, Caroline, Sprinter Sacre made his bumper debut at Ascot in February

2010, just four months after arriving at Henderson's yard. The Ascot race was won, as was another bumper two months later at Ayr. Asked to race over two and a half miles for the first and only time on his hurdling debut the following November, the then four-year-old was beaten into second. Not long after the defeat, he had 'muck pouring out of his nostrils'. Victories at Ffos Las and Ascot followed. Then sent to the Cheltenham Festival for the first time, and discarded by Barry Geraghty in favour of Spirit Son, Sprinter Sacre weakened to finish third in the Supreme Novices' Hurdle. In the moments that followed, Tony McCoy recommended a breathing operation.

Henderson listened while telling more than one person that in 12 months' time he expected to be standing in the place reserved for the winner of the Arkle. 'He was always a brilliant jumper – he's been on springs all his life,' says Henderson, while the trainer's amateur Nico de Boinville, Sprinter Sacre's rider at home since day one, vividly remembers the horse's first session schooling over fences late last October. 'He was electric,' says de Boinville. 'He went out on his own and pinged five fences, one after the other, jumping like an experienced chaser. Barry Geraghty looked at me afterwards and just said: 'Phwoar!' The word that comes to mind when I think of him is freak. He's a pure monster of a horse and it's amazing how much he has strengthened up since he first came into the yard. He was a backward baby when he came to us but now he's totally different. I would say there's still a bit more to come as well.'

As we have seen this season there is plenty there already. With Geraghty on duty at Cheltenham, de Boinville's housemate David Bass had the pleasure of being in the saddle for the horse's chasing debut at Doncaster, where immaculate jumping was the hallmark of a 24-length success. Eighteen days later, Sprinter Sacre kept Kempton buzzing on the day after Kauto Star's fifth King George triumph by thrashing Peddlers Cross with a display that had star quality stamped all over it, so much so that Henderson briefly contemplated

“

When he took to fences he was a spectacular, spectacular jumper. He was one of those horses who go up a gear when they get to fences. He was mighty, very strong, very exuberant. He went into a fence five lengths down and landed three in front and they christened him 'The Black Aeroplane'.

NICKY HENDERSON

Working in sunshine, Nico de Boinville and Sprinter Sacre at home on the gallops

making an entry for the Queen Mother Champion Chase. He decided against such a move and instead pressed on to the Arkle via Newbury's Game Spirit Chase, in which Sprinter Sacre won without coming off the bridle, prompting Geraghty to describe him as 'a Ferrari without brakes'.

'I thought he was stunning at Newbury and then at Cheltenham he was frightening,' says Henderson. 'Winning the Arkle was a relief really. Out of our whole team he had to be my best chance. Given the way he had been hyped up nothing other than an outstanding performance would have been good enough.' Would the performance have been good enough to stop stable companion Finian's Rainbow from winning the Champion Chase? 'There's no point in trying to guess and we won both races, so it worked out perfectly,' says the trainer,

CHELTENHAM
Racing Post Arkle Challenge Trophy Chase

2009-10 | 2010-11 | 2011-12 | 2012-13

FEB | MAR | APR | NOV | DEC | JAN | FEB | MAR | APR | NOV | DEC | JAN | FEB | MAR | APR | NOV | DEC | JAN | FEB | MAR | APR

who admits a clash between the two horses is more than possible next March.

'I'd rather have two runners in next year's Champion Chase than none,' he says. 'If they do meet in the Champion Chase, then so be it. Barry would have a dilemma on his hands. I wouldn't.' Henderson also expects further progress from the Aintree-bound six-year-old who could undergo another breathing operation before he starts his second season over fences. 'His wind is always in the back of my mind and it's possible it might need redoing,' says Henderson. 'We often redo that sort of procedure at the beginning of the season. We'll have a look at him when he comes back and decide if we think a little more maintenance is necessary. Whether we do or we don't, he undoubtedly improved enormously from last season to this season and you would be disappointed if there wasn't more to come.'

If there is, further Cheltenham Festival celebrations are surely inevitable. 'He's an amazing horse with the most wonderful temperament,' says Caroline Mould, whose post-Arkle delight was heightened by the arrival of a link to her horse's past. 'After he won at Newbury I said to Raymond how lovely it would be to know more about where he came from. Then, after the Arkle three diminutive Frenchmen pitched up. One of them turned out to be the breeder. I was really choked.' As was Christophe Masle. 'He was ecstatic,' says Raymond Mould. 'He doesn't speak a word of English, so we didn't have much of a conversation but he was clearly over the moon.' He still is. Masle, the small man with the small voice, describes Sprinter Sacre as a horse with 'beaucoup, beaucoup, beaucoup de qualité'. Reflecting on his trip to Cheltenham, he adds: 'The day of the Arkle was magnificent, incredible and amazing. It was my first time at Cheltenham and seeing him win gave me enormous joy.'

Back home in the beating heart of France's AQPS country and reunited with his sheep and cows, Masle has once again been dabbling with the breeding of racehorses. 'I hope that next year we will have another brother or sister for Sprinter

Sprinter Sacre is given a handy lead by Australia Day at Aintree in the Maghull Novices' Chase, April 2012

Sacre,' he reveals, explaining that on 24 March Fatima was once again covered by Network.

On this occasion, Dark Moondancer was nowhere to be seen.

Aintree was the last date of the novice season and it completed a tour de force. 'Unbeatable' is a dangerous word but Sprinter Sacre was beginning to look very close to it.

We have reached the point where the only person who gets no pleasure from watching Sprinter Sacre in action is Nicky Henderson. For the rest of us it is a rare joy. To see this extraordinary young talent, so wonderfully enthusiastic, so incredibly talented, soaring over his fences and humiliating those who dare to take him on, has become one of this sport's great delights. Yesterday Caroline Mould's superstar novice wowed us once again when cantering to a 13-length Grade 1 success

AINTREE
John Smith's Maghull Novices' Chase

2009–10 | 2010–11 | 2011–12 | 2012–13

FEB | MAR | APR | NOV | DEC | JAN | FEB | MAR | APR | NOV | DEC | JAN | FEB | MAR | APR | NOV | DEC | JAN | FEB | MAR | APR

in the John Smith's Maghull Chase. However, while we were wowed, the trainer was worried.

'It's over, thank God,' said Henderson. 'It's like that now because anything bar perfection will disappoint everybody. He's spectacular and it's a joy to watch – when it's over. I said to Caroline it's been fun until now but it's not fun anymore, it's frightening.'

While Henderson's reaction was understandable, the only ones yesterday entitled to feel terror were runner-up Toubab, Kudu Country and Australia Day, the three horses who saw the Racing Post Arkle Chase hero speed away midway down the back stretch when Barry Geraghty decided that the cross noseband, fitted to Sprinter Sacre for the first time, was not having the desired restraining effect. Geraghty let his mount go and his mount went, very fast and very far into the distance.

'He was brilliant,' said Geraghty. 'I could only stay behind Australia Day for so long and I was going to have to let him roll at some stage. He was very fresh today, perhaps overly fresh, because he hadn't done a lot since Cheltenham. Every jump is like a bungee jump – I've never ridden a horse with so much scope. He's a monster.'

Henderson added: 'We don't have to think whether he's better than Finian's Rainbow at the moment. We have a long summer when the horses can relax and we can dream.'

And then, come the autumn, Henderson can start worrying all over again. *(Lee Mottershead)*

2
ZENITH

PREVIOUS SPREAD: Barry Geraghty and Sprinter Sacre reach the summit as they complete a rarefied treble at Punchestown

THE 2012/2013 season was to see Sprinter Sacre at his absolute zenith. No one who was around at the time will ever forget the sight of him in full stride. But the delight was magnified in that this supremacy was already so keenly anticipated. Before he had even started there was a wonderful collective licking of lips.

In hindsight, it's hard to imagine any opposition being considered serious in this, Sprinter's season of seasons. But his first outing in the Tingle Creek at Sandown in December was thought to be just that. Sanctuaire had looked dazzlingly brilliant in his three chase wins the previous season culminating in a 17 lengths Celebration Chase thrashing of Somersby on this same Sandown track in April.

Beforehand *Racing Post* added to its breathless preview with a boxing style 'tale of the tape'.

TALE OF THE TAPE

Barry Geraghty	JOCKEY	Ruby Walsh
Nicky Henderson	TRAINER	Paul Nicholls
Caroline Mould	OWNER	Potensis Ltd/Chris Giles
17.1½	HEIGHT (hands)	16.2
539	WEIGHT (approx kg)	520
April 23, 2006	BORN	May 15, 2006
French	BRED	French
£194,972	PRIZE-MONEY	£154,576
169	OFFICIAL RATING	166
176	RACING POST RATING	168
5	CHASE STARTS	3
5	CHASE WINS	3
2	GRADE 1 WINS	0
0/0	SANDOWN RECORD	2/3
13.2	AVERAGE WINNING DISTANCE OVER FENCES	24.7

SPRINTER SACRE

PROS Looked a superstar in the making with five wins over fences last season that elevated him to within 4lb of Finian's Rainbow, and more improvement is likely.

CONS Has won on soft but at his best on a quicker surface and as a keen-going horse the ground could test his depths of stamina

SANCTUAIRE

PROS Announced himself as a top prospect when destroying Somersby in the Celebration Chase to earn a rating higher than any previous Nicholls novice chaser.

CONS Has proved temperamental in the past and wasn't able to build as successfully as hoped on a hurdles career that included a Fred Winter victory at the Cheltenham Festival.

SANDOWN
Sportingbet Tingle Creek Chase

2009-10 | 2010-11 | 2011-12 | 2012-13
FEB | MAR | APR | NOV | DEC | JAN | FEB | MAR | APR | NOV | DEC | JAN | FEB | MAR | APR | NOV | DEC | JAN | FEB | MAR | APR

Last season's outstanding two-mile novice chaser Sprinter Sacre faces the first test of his candidacy for the champion's crown held by stablemate Finian's Rainbow when he makes one of the season's most eagerly anticipated returns to action at Sandown today.

Jump racing loves its established stars, but after just one season over fences Sprinter Sacre's stature already towers above those who have been campaigning for longer and he puts that reputation on the line in the Tingle Creek Chase.

In the course of a five-race unbeaten run over fences, Sprinter Sacre defeated Peddlers Cross at Kempton, Cue Card in the Racing Post Arkle and added another victory at Aintree in such impressive fashion that he is already being talked of in superstar terms.

No better than evens for the Champion Chase at Cheltenham in March, he comes to a race which so many great stars have won trying to put down an early marker. His absence from a planned prep race at Cheltenham last month has only heightened the anticipation and, despite missing that engagement, Henderson says his star is more than ready for the clash with Sanctuaire.

'It wasn't that he desperately needed a race, but it was there and I thought we might use it,' he said. 'He has done plenty. I'm not saying he won't come on for it – they all will at this time of the year – but it wasn't imperative to have a race.

'We don't know what he'll be like in soft ground. Cheltenham was very soft and it was too close to this to risk if he had got into a slog. If he didn't like the ground at Cheltenham he might have finished up getting a race that he didn't need. He's been working nicely and schooling like he always does. Touch wood, everything's gone according to plan.'

Paul Nicholls has made this contest his own in recent years and he is not about to concede the Grade 1 prize lightly just yet, not even to a horse of the calibre of Sprinter Sacre.

The champion trainer's record stands at eight wins from 13 runnings of Sandown's flagship jumps race, six of which came

"

I remember getting a bit too excited about Master Minded and he let us down a bit. Sprinter Sacre is a little in the same mould, as at the beginning of his career he looked as though he was going to be the next Arkle.

It's still a possibility. He's exciting and let's hope he doesn't have to run in a bog. I think he'll be better on racing ground. He's a speed merchant who jumps very quickly.

There was a moment on his last start when I thought things weren't going as well as they should have been, but he's obviously a very exciting horse and the most exciting race of the Festival for me is the Champion Chase.

WILLIE CARSON
Five-time champion Flat jockey

"

He could be one of the best we've seen for 30 years. He's got so much natural speed and is a very good horse.

PHILIP HOBBS
Trainer

Sanctuaire was always going to go a pace that would test anybody's fitness and that was a right, screaming Sandown two-mile chase. Barry said the ground was as soft as he would ever want to go on but he's just class. I would say he will go Victor Chandler and Cheltenham.

NICKY HENDERSON

in consecutive years with Kauto Star, Master Minded and Twist Magic securing two apiece.

A year ago Nicholls had to settle for second when Kauto Stone was outpointed by Sizing Europe but he has regrouped and emerged with yet another potential star in Sanctuaire, who has made rapid strides since switching to fences culminating in a 17-length defeat of Somersby over course and distance in April.

Without hesitation the trainer nominated this race as the horse's next start even then knowing it was likely to set up a clash with the brilliant Sprinter Sacre. It might not be as one-sided as the betting suggests with Sanctuaire only 3lb inferior on official ratings and the smart form shown by Nicholls' team this term, notably Al Ferof and Silviniaco Conti, is a prime source of confidence.

'He's fit and well but it's a tough challenge,' said Nicholls. 'I have no idea how good he is. We can't tell until they run but it's a bit like Silviniaco Conti when he ran in the Charlie Hall. We hoped he'd improve. All our second-season horses have improved and if he has, he has a chance. It's going to be a challenge to beat Sprinter Sacre. *(Jon Lees)*

The racing world may have been holding it's breath but when the race came it was not even close:

Nicky Henderson had spent the week being petrified by the prospect of putting Sprinter Sacre through the stiffest test of his career, but he needn't have been concerned as the champion chaser-elect produced an imperious comeback display yesterday.

Sprinter Sacre and Sanctuaire went into the Sportingbet Tingle Creek Chase barely separated on BHA figures but in reality the gulf in class was huge, as last season's Racing Post Arkle Chase winner handed out a thorough beating to Paul Nicholls' best ever novice chaser.

The nearest thing jump racing has to Frankel, now that Kauto Star is in retirement, coasted over the line 15 lengths clear of Kumbeshwar, with a tired Sanctuaire third, to win with his head in his chest.

In so doing he stretched his unbeaten run over fences to six in front of an elated crowd of 11,100, but not before Sprinter Sacre had been asked searching questions by Ruby Walsh on Sanctuaire.

At the track where Sanctuaire had taken the Celebration Chase by 17 lengths, Walsh set out to make all the running. At one point they held an eight-length advantage, but Sprinter Sacre and Barry Geraghty gradually made up the deficit and, by the time they reached the Pond fence, victory was assured for Caroline Mould's champion.

Sprinter Sacre clears the first in the hotly anticipated Tingle Creek at Sandown in 2012

Nicky Henderson regaling the latest outstanding exploits of his superstar to the press in Cheltenham's winner's enclosure

allowed him his head shortly after heading on to the far side, and it was soon game over for his rivals. He soared over the fifth-last and didn't have to be nearly fully extended up the home straight.

This is unquestionably the best 2m chaser since the golden era of Moscow Flyer and there must be every chance he can better the best RPR achieved by that rival of 182, as he firmly has age on his side being only a 7yo still. Next up will be the Champion Chase back here in March and it's nigh on impossible to see him losing his unbeaten record over fences in that, with ante-post odds of 2-5 in places perfectly reasonable. Indeed, he is flawless.

So to the Festival with the cautious thought that such praise can be dangerous and Cheltenham is the most demanding of places to match words with deeds. But after this Champion Chase, all comparisons had to pale.

Keen to gain insight from the horse's mouth, Clare Balding has a word with the uniquely charismatic Sprinter Sacre while visiting Seven Barrows for Channel 4's *The Morning Line* in January 2013

SENSATIONAL SACRE

Extraterrestrial Sprinter barely out of second gear as he cruises home in a Champion Chase procession.

Nothing short of sensational would have sufficed, and Sprinter Sacre was nothing short of sensational. Nicky Henderson was a bundle of nerves and described watching the race unfold as 'hell', but for the rest of us it was among the most sublime experiences we have been privileged to witness on a racecourse.

The 19 lengths by which Sprinter Sacre scored was by no means the Queen Mother Champion Chase's widest winning margin – Master Minded scored by an identical distance as recently as 2008 and former greats such as Dunkirk, Crisp and Badsworth Boy all won by even further – but surely none of them treated yardsticks as talented as 2011 winner Sizing Europe with quite such disdain.

GUINNESS GRANDSTAND
GUINNESS
AT THE RACES
5

"

He's a horse everyone wants to be involved with. He's a huge talent – he jumps, travels, stays and has so much class. He's got everything you need in a two-mile chaser as he jumps at speed and travels so well in his races. It's hard to see how you can beat him.

RICHARD JOHNSON
Jockey

Sprinter Sacre is a beautiful horse, a natural jumper. I have ridden some brilliant horses over the years but it is the ease with which he does it that sets him apart.

BARRY GERAGHTY

PREVIOUS SPREAD: Sprinter Sacre lands over the second last fence at Cheltenham in splendid isolation as Barry Geraghty steers him to his first Queen Mother Champion Chase in 2013

ABOVE: With Sprinter Sacre now dubbed 'The Black Aeroplane', fans get into the spirit

Following another virtually flawless display, Sprinter Sacre simply sauntered away from Sizing Europe approaching the final bend, the pair of them having already left classy rivals standing as they started down the hill. The winner was never remotely off the bridle and, while only time will tell, one cannot help thinking the hastily calculated 188 revealed by BHA head of handicapping Phil Smith – still 5lb short of Kauto Star's peak – may well turn out to seriously underestimate him. The Racing Post Rating of 190 is our highest figure ever recorded at the Festival.

Barry Geraghty, who enjoyed a superb association with dual Champion Chase winner Moscow Flyer, was reluctant to make comparisons, but admitted that while Moscow Flyer was 'a super horse', Sprinter Sacre is 'just unbelievable and oozes class'.

'I've never ridden a horse that does it all so easily,' he added. 'He's like Pele, who used to do it all so easily because his speed and power and skill gave him the time to do it.' He is only seven and yet to be troubled in eight starts over fences and we can look forward to one more sight of Sprinter Sacre this year, in the Champion Chase at Punchestown.

'That was probably the worst five minutes of my life, but so long as Barry enjoyed it that's great,' said Henderson as he waited for Sprinter Sacre to return to the winner's enclosure. 'That's a proper racehorse, doing what steeplechasing is all about. He's got that wow factor about him, and he knows it too. What he looks like and what he does at home is one thing, but what he does out there is totally unique.'

Sprinter Sacre has evidently always displayed extraordinary natural talent. Henderson said: 'He doesn't hide his light under a bushel and he doesn't do anything by halves. He knows he's good and he likes to tell everyone. He's almost the perfect racehorse. We are very lucky to have him. It's a true privilege.' He added: 'I'm sure he'll get further, but would you ever dare ask him? He could easily go to Punchestown, because he's had only three races this season, then I think he'd follow a similar programme next season.'

3.20 RACE 4 — *Sportingbet Queen Mother Champion Chase (Grade 1) (Class 1)* — CH4 — *Winner £208,300.32* — **2m Old**

£350,000 guaranteed **For** 5yo+ which are allotted a rating of 130 or more by the BHA Head of Handicapping following a review of the horses entered and after taking account of races run up to and including March 6th. (Horses which are not qualified for a rating in Great Britain, Ireland or France may also be entered. Such horses may be eligible providing the Handicapper is satisfied that the horse's racecourse performances up to and including March 6th would merit a minimum rating of 130. The decision of the BHA Head of Handicapping shall be final) **Weights** 11st 10lb **Allowances** mares 7lb **Entries** 17 pay £435 **1st Forfeit** 9 pay £870 **2nd Forfeit** 1 pay £17500 **Confirmed** 10 pay £435 **Penalty value 1st** £208,300.32 **2nd** £78,162.91 **3rd** £39,136.32 **4th** £19,495.01 **5th** £9,802.37 **6th** £4,901.18

No.	Form	Horse / Breeding / Trainer & Owner	Age / Wt / Jockey	RPR
1	211/4-5	**MAIL DE BIEVRE** (FR) 32 *b g Cadoudal-Coyote Davis* **Tom George**[2] P E Atkinson	8 11-10 **Paddy Brennan**	154
2	111-314	**SANCTUAIRE** (FR) TTF46 D5 C1 *b/br g Kendor-Biblique* **Paul Nicholls** Potensis Limited & Chris Giles	7 11-10 **R Walsh**	175
3	21-1111	**SIZING EUROPE** (IRE) TTF38 D10 C1 CD2 *b g Pistolet Bleu-Jennie Dun* **Henry de Bromhead (IRE)** Ann & Alan Potts Partnership	11 11-10 **A E Lynch**	178
4	4172-34	**SOMERSBY** (IRE) TTF25 D4 *b g Second Empire-Back To Roost* **Mick Channon** Mrs T P Radford	p 9 11-10 **Dominic Elsworth**	171
5	1111-11	**SPRINTER SACRE** (FR) TTF46 D9 C1 CD1 *b/br g Notwork Fatima III* **Nicky Henderson** Mrs Caroline Mould	7 11-10 **Barry Geraghty**	182
6	35/1-57	**TATANIANO** (FR) TTF103 D3 C1 CD1 *b g Sassanian-Rosa Carola* **Richard Rowe**[1] The Stewart Family	9 11-10 **Andrew Thornton**	157
7	25-2141	**WISHFULL THINKING** TTF32 C1 CD1 *ch g Alflora-Poussetiere Deux* **Philip Hobbs** Mrs Diana L Whateley	t 10 11-10 **Richard Johnson**	169

2012 (8 ran) **Finian's Rainbow** Nicky Henderson 9 11-10 4/1 Barry Geraghty RPR175

BETTING FORECAST: 1-4 Sprinter Sacre, 5 Sizing Europe, 14 Mail de Bievre, 20 Sanctuaire, Wishfull Thinking, 25 Somersby, 100 Tataniano.

Sizing Europe beat the rest decisively, despite a scare when he lost his hind legs crossing the woodchip path after the third-last. Jockey Andrew Lynch confirmed he tripped but admitted: 'The race was over and I couldn't use that as an excuse. Sprinter Sacre is some horse. It was worth taking a shot at him to find out how good he is, and it just shows you that he really is a proper horse. My lad still ran well.'

Trainer Henry de Bromhead was as proud of Sizing Europe as he was unstinting in his praise of the winner, who he said was 'phenomenal'. He added: 'We'll see if we come back next year. Our horse was still second in a Champion Chase with some good horses behind him. He's still good. It was the right decision to run. We did everything to go out to win the race and I thought he jumped brilliantly. He did everything brilliantly and was just beaten by a very special horse on the day.' *(Graham Dench)*

Sprinter Sacre's 'Wow' factor now spread way beyond racing professionals. As in the days of Arkle and Desert Orchid racegoers would throng the rails just to get a glimpse of their hero. At Cheltenham Lee Mottershead went with them.

THE BRAD PITT OF RACEHORSES

In normal circumstances the place to be after the RSA Chase would be by the winner's enclosure, awaiting the return of the RSA Chase winner. These, though, are not normal circumstances.

Lord Windermere is greeted by the hearty ovation that every Festival hero receives but, had it not been for the horse who comes next, it would surely have been louder. Many of the winner's enclosure regulars have instead hotfooted it to the pre-parade ring, tucked into a corner of the racecourse, almost always ignored by the majority of Festival faithful. Today is different because today there is something out of the ordinary to see.

There are more people around the pre-parade ring than attend many race meetings. 'This is the busiest I've seen it,' says annual member Anil Patel. 'I've made my way over just to see him. I'm not a horse person, but even I can recognise he looks special. His skin just gleams. You can tell this is an absolute star. He's like the Brad Pitt of racehorses. They keep calling him the Frankel of the jumps world but he doesn't need to be compared to any other horse. He is Sprinter Sacre.'

He is indeed. He is also the biggest equine star in the sport and 1-4 favourite for the Sportingbet Queen Mother Champion Chase next year. 'I've not had a bet and you don't need to,' says Surrey's Dan Abraham. 'You need only to hear how loudly the winners are cheered in to realise that for a lot of people here betting is secondary to watching very good horses.'

The horse we then see must be one of the best there has been, and certainly the finest two-mile chaser for decades, a spectacular creature being followed by fans thousands of miles from his home. Kevin Panyandee, a very long-distance visitor,

Barry Geraghty smiles for the cameras as Sprinter Sacre pulls up after an exhilarating display. His 'rivals' are still nowhere to be seen

is one such devotee. 'He's even starting to be well known in Mauritius and I came all the way from there just to see him,' says Panyandee. 'He's a big phenomenon. He's a blend of Usain Bolt and Mo Farah, a combination of incredible speed and stamina. He is so beautiful. When you see him, it is like looking at a picture.'

Not merely a picture. This is a masterpiece.

It was in every sense a day for the history books. The challenge for our writers was to record it in words worthy of their subject. It was a challenge that Alastair Down picked up with relish.

Just before half past three yesterday afternoon the map of the known jumping world was redrawn forever when Sprinter Sacre took the sport into hitherto uncharted territory with a gasp-inducing masterclass the like of which has never previously been seen over two miles of fast-flown steeplechase fences.

“

He's the most exciting two-miler we've seen for a very long time, and the race that immediately springs to mind whenever I think about him is his Newbury win at the beginning of the year.

I remember it so well because Barnbrook Again, whom I rode, held the two-mile track record until that day. Sprinter Sacre beat that time by fully four seconds, even though he was eased right down on the run-in, having been hard on the bridle at the last fence.

I know we are talking about different eras, and that Barnbrook Again carried 12st 7lb, whereas Sprinter Sacre only had 11st 5lb on his back, but I thought 'this horse has got to be special', and he is.

BRENDAN POWELL
Trainer and former Grand National-winning jockey

Rarely has the Festival air crackled with such anticipatory excitement as in the minutes during which the field made its way out to parade before the purists' ultimate examination that is the Champion Chase. And it is almost impossible to convey how awesome Sprinter Sacre looked – coat gleaming like a polished mahogany table, all power and muscle coiled under Barry Geraghty and, most extraordinary of all, with an air of pure threat and lethality about him.

There is something almost scary about Sprinter Sacre, something not quite suitable for the children. To this increasingly seasoned observer he is the first X-rated chaser. As the seconds ticked away to the off, debate on the press balcony concluded that we wanted to see Sprinter Sacre win by at least 15 lengths and for the admirable Sizing Europe to finish second, giving gold-plating to the form. The moment of revelation came as they began the descent of the hill. Suddenly the two central characters in the drama simply ghosted 15 lengths clear, the issue between them alone and the chaff blown away to a zone of utter irrelevance.

Sprinter Sacre was upsides Sizing Europe three from home and then there came one of those marvellous moments when pure class cut in and he eased clear. It was not some dramatic quickening or the result of Geraghty doing anything as impertinent as asking him to go to work – it was just the race-changing exertion of his incalculable superiority.

Five lengths clear two out, he simply processed away, the king coming to his coronation and his admiring subjects in the stands unleashed a crashing adulatory roar – tens of thousands of voices speaking as one – as he touched down, safe, secure and supreme on the landing side of the last.

Still barely doing more than going through the motions and never under the slightest pressure, he stretched 19 lengths clear up the run-in, leaving the abiding impression that despite having annihilated his field there was any amount still in untapped reserve.

Many of those who pack the Cheltenham enclosures at the Festival do so in the fervent hope it will be during their time,

on their watch, that horses of genuine wonder will come along and change forever our idea of the possible. Sprinter Sacre did just that yesterday and the reception he received from the faithful as he and Geraghty came back down the horse-walk mingled admiration with excitement and no small touch of awe.

The awaiting winner's enclosure was under siege with the steppings rammed by those wanting to feast their eyes on this new

Sarwar Mohammed and Barry Geraghty mirror celebrations as they are greeted by an awestruck crowd entering Cheltenham's winners' enclosure

“

I have to finally admit that he's at the top of my pile but I'm not going to compare him with other people's horses. I'm not saying he won't go to Punchestown and I'm not throwing it completely out of the window. The original plan was to go there. I've always promised I'll take him to Ireland one day. We'll think about it but if he doesn't go there it will be the Tingle Creek next and then the same as this season. I think that's as far as he needs to go and we wouldn't think about a King George at this particular moment.

NICKY HENDERSON

Among the heaving hoards at Aintree was a small Irishman of a certain age, here in Liverpool with his wife for their annual visit to the Grand National meeting. As a man who had known Arkle better than most, he was eminently capable of passing judgement on the horse whose remarkable talent had once again beggared belief. Paddy Woods recognised what he had seen. So did we all.

Through the most celebrated career in jump racing history, Woods was the man who rode Arkle each and every morning. He knows how an outstanding horse feels in the hands and he knows how an outstanding horse looks to the eye. After Sprinter Sacre had humiliated not one but two exceptional rivals in Cue Card and Flemenstar, the human link to the greatest jumps horse there has ever been delivered a mighty plaudit. ‘He's definitely the best I've seen since Arkle,’ said Woods. ‘He looks magnificent and is the complete package. He has everything.’

Among the everything that Sprinter Sacre possesses is the ability to stay two and a half miles. Prior to yesterday's John Smith's Melling Chase, we knew from two exhilarating displays at the Cheltenham Festival that he was untouchable over two miles. Now we know he is untouchable over further.

For a moment turning for home Barry Geraghty was forced to move a muscle, but a moment is all it was. From there to the line racing's most precious equine asset was sublime, first eyeballing Ryanair Chase winner Cue Card, who had made much of the running, before sauntering clear for a four-and-a-half-length success at prohibitive, but ultimately generous, odds of 1-3. A long 19 lengths back in third was Ireland's bright hope Flemenstar, humbled but with reputation intact.

‘It's a joy now it's over, but during the race my eyes were shut,’ said trainer Nicky Henderson, whose 2012 Melling winner Finian's Rainbow ran his best race of the season in fourth. ‘We had to make up a bit of ground on a very good horse in Cue Card, but it didn't seem too difficult. This fellow

loves what he's doing and I'm conscious he's something to be enjoyed. I'm the custodian, and lucky to be the custodian of a spectacular horse. I must try to bring him back to the racecourse as often as I can.'

There is a possibility the next racecourse trip could come as soon as the opening day of the Punchestown Festival. 'I've promised I'll take him to Ireland one day,' said Henderson, who seemed less keen on a further step up in trip for the William Hill King George VI Chase, for which the sponsors make him 6-4 favourite. 'We wouldn't think about a King George at this particular moment,' he said, adding: 'I think today's trip is as far as he needs to go.'

At this trip he is magnificent, as Geraghty knows best. 'He did what we thought he'd do,' he said. 'The distance was no

The power of take-off, Sprinter Sacre leaves another indelible impression, this time at Aintree in the Melling Chase 2013

concern to me. We've come to expect great performances from him and we got a great performance. It's just brilliant. He's a great horse and I love riding him.'

For Geraghty, the whole Sprinter Sacre experience is pure pleasure. Not so for Henderson. Nor for owner Caroline Mould. 'You always want a horse like this, but when you have one it's a very different ball game,' she said. 'I had the window down in the car coming to Aintree because I thought I was going to be sick. You have reservations every time he runs, as it's obvious he's become public property. That brings a huge pressure.'

Asked if she feared her horse might one day be beaten, Mould nodded. 'I do, but I'm fairly fatalistic,' she said. Those

The appreciative Liverpool crowd flock to see the newly crowned champion chaser

connected with the vanquished must view the possibility of the sacred one ever being defeated as extremely doubtful.

'I'm as proud as hell of Cue Card,' said rider Joe Tizzard, while trainer-father Colin, who will now send his stable star on holiday, observed: 'Sprinter Sacre is the best I've seen and to me would stay any trip. I don't think I'd be in a hurry to take him on again. Once a year is enough!'

As it almost certainly will be for the Punchestown-bound Flemenstar. 'The plain and simple truth is that he just was not good enough,' said trainer Peter Casey's son Francis. 'There are no excuses. He'll win plenty of Grade 1s in Ireland and nine times out of ten he'd have won that race.'

3.05 RACE 3 — *John Smith's Melling Chase (Grade 1) (Class 1)* — *Winner £112,540* — **CH4** — **2m4f Mildmay**

£200,000 guaranteed **For** 5yo+ **Weights** 11st 10lb **Allowances** mares 7lb **Entries** 9 pay £1000 **Penalty value 1st** £112,540 **2nd** £42,400 **3rd** £21,220 **4th** £10,600 **5th** £5,320 **6th** £2,660

1	12-1511	**CUE CARD** TTF 22 D2 C1 *b g King's Theatre-Wicked Crack* **Colin Tizzard** Mrs Jean R Bishop	7 11-10 **Joe Tizzard**	180
2	1211-46	**FINIAN'S RAINBOW** (IRE) TTF 48 D1 C1 CD1 *b g Tiraaz-Trinity Gale* **Nicky Henderson** Michael Buckley	10 11-10 **A P McCoy**	179
3	11-1132	**FLEMENSTAR** (IRE) TTF 55 BF D3 *b g Flemensfirth-Different Dee* **Peter Casey (IRE)** Stephen Curran	8 11-10 **A E Lynch**	175
4	13-1253	**FOR NON STOP** (IRE) TTF 22 D2 CD1 *b g Alderbrook-Lost Link* **Nick Williams** Potensis Limited & Chris Giles	8 11-10 **Noel Fehily**	171
5	-R3042R	**MAD MOOSE** (IRE) 22 D1 *ch g Presenting-Sheshollystar* **Nigel Twiston-Davies** Middleham Park Racing XXXV & Partner	b 9 11-10 **Sam Twiston-Davies**	160
6	111-111	**SPRINTER SACRE** (FR) TTF 23 C1 *b/br g Network-Fatima III* **Nicky Henderson** Mrs Caroline Mould	7 11-10 **Barry Geraghty**	194

2012 (8 ran) **Finian's Rainbow** Nicky Henderson 9 11-10 13/8F Barry Geraghty RPR172

BETTING FORECAST: 1-3 Sprinter Sacre, 9-2 Flemenstar, 11-2 Cue Card, 10 Finian's Rainbow, 25 For Non Stop, 100 Mad Moose.

Then, just as compatriot Paddy Woods had done, Casey harked back to another age. 'After 50 years,' he said, 'you're finally getting your own back on us for Arkle kicking the s*** out of you.'

And no matter where you hail from, watching him kick is a wonderful delight. *(Lee Mottershead)*

RACING POST RATINGS: Another jaw-dropping display from the seemingly flawless Sprinter Sacre (190+) and, although the winning distance was nowhere near that of his runaway Champion Chase success, it was probably every bit as good a run.

It's anybody's guess how much he had in hand, but it's not unrealistic to think he was value for at least a double-digit winning margin from a peak form Cue Card (178), who is judged to have run a personal best figure in defeat.

There's a case for rating the race a fair bit higher through the remainder, but both Flemenstar (161) and Finian's Rainbow (159) look to have run upwards of 10lb below their best.

TOP CHASERS THIS SEASON

RPR	*Horse*
190	**Sprinter Sacre**
181	Bobs Worth
178	Cue Card
175	Silviniaco Conti
174	Long Run
174	Sir Des Champs
174	Tidal Bay
173	Sizing Europe
172	Al Ferof
171	Flemenstar

PREVIOUS SPREAD: A proud Nicky Henderson presents Sprinter Sacre to the press

The jumping world was now reeling with the possibilities. So on the Monday after Aintree we gave one of our 'Expert Juries' the question: 'What Next For Sprinter Sacre?'

RICHARD BIRCH, Reporter

There is something intrinsically beautiful about watching Sprinter Sacre. It is the natural exuberance with which he travels and the extraordinary scope he has at his fences. It is the enticing suspicion that no rival is capable of getting him off the bridle over trips between two and three miles.

He simply toyed with top-class opponents upped in distance yesterday. It is impossible to know how much he had in reserve, but it looked an awful lot.

The fact he settles so much better now surely means connections will seriously consider the King George. If any bookmaker offered 4-5 for that race there would be a stampede.

He could be remembered as a multiple winner of the Champion Chase and King George.

TOM KERR, Reporter

As one of the dwindling band of idiots who yesterday thought there was some way Sprinter Sacre could be beaten, I am now obviously reluctant to say there's anything he can't do. Three miles, the Gold Cup, trigonometry, interior decoration – who knows?

The nonchalant way he dismissed one of the finest steeplechasers around, Cue Card, was astonishing. It was like watching Lionel Messi torment a leaden-footed Championship defence, except Sprinter Sacre was playing Champions League-standard opposition.

Two futures now lie ahead of Sprinter Sacre. He can venture further down the path he is on, into the uncharted uplands of three miles and more, or return back to his old stomping grounds of two miles. I hope for the former, for if Sprinter Sacre does venture into the unknown I expect he'll sweep all before him like an equine Alexander.

Who's the boss? Sprinter Sacre and Nicky Henderson, a close partnership

ED QUIGLEY, Form Analyst

On paper at least, this was supposed to be Sprinter Sacre's toughest race. The way he made a mockery of some top-class rivals on his first start over fences at two and a half miles can only make you shower him with superlatives.

The manner in which he won suggests there are all sorts of avenues open to him now. The two-mile division looks to be almost too easy for him and so it wouldn't be inconceivable that connections consider a tilt at the King George. He has such a natural cruising speed and with plenty of stamina in his pedigree he could easily get the trip.

Connections have the reassurance that they can drop back to mop up the top two-mile races if things don't work out over further, so why not have a go?

Sprinter Sacre (right) and Nico de Boinville out on the hill at Seven Barrows

To all racing fans' delight Sprinter Sacre's 'Annus Mirabilis' was not over. With belief and great goodwill he was now sent over to Ireland for the Punchestown Festival and the sort of reception usually reserved for visiting US Presidents.

It was another triumph and the greatest of days. In hindsight it was probably also one of the greatest of strains for, although Sprinter duly delivered, the first signs of future fragility were there if anyone had bothered to notice.

But only a hardened pessimist could worry when such a champion had come to town.

A perfect ten out of ten over fences, a third Grade 1 chase success in six weeks and the first horse since Istabraq to win at the Cheltenham, Aintree and Punchestown Festivals.

The positive effect of having a superstar like Sprinter Sacre on the jump racing scene is incalculable, but it was given some visual context by the sight of a record first-day crowd of 18,607 cheering him back in after his victory in the Boylesports.com Champion Chase in scenes the likes of which have not been witnessed at the Punchestown Festival since Dawn Run beat Buck House in The Match in 1986.

Winning rider Barry Geraghty provided his personal comparison when saying he had not experienced anything like it

LEFT: Nicky Henderson's travelling head lass Sarah Shreeve puts Sprinter Sacre through his paces as they prepare for Punchestown

BELOW RIGHT: Barry Geraghty and Sprinter Sacre canter to the start at Punchestown

BELOW LEFT: Parading in front of packed Punchestown grandstands before the 2013 Boylesports Champion Chase

since watching Desert Orchid win the Irish Grand National at Fairyhouse when the jockey was just ten years of age.

But it wasn't plain sailing. A stop-start gallop was set by former champion Sizing Europe and the old warrior managed to take Sprinter Sacre to the last and forced him to be at least shaken up for a few strides before proper order was

AT THE RACES

PREVIOUS SPREAD: For the first time since his hurdling days, Sprinter Sacre is made to battle by Sizing Europe

ABOVE: Barry Geraghty acknowledges a grateful Irish crowd. The Festival Treble is complete

restored. The 19 lengths from Cheltenham were narrowed to a mere five and a half lengths this time, but it was obvious the 11-year-old Sizing Europe had run his heart out while the new young champion had suffered no more than a minor inconvenience.

'It was tougher today, but he was at his best at Cheltenham, he wasn't quite as sharp at Aintree and he's probably not as sharp today,' said trainer Nicky Henderson. 'You have to have

PUNCHESTOWN
Boylesports.com Champion Chase

2009-10 | 2010-11 | 2011-12 | 2012-13

FEB | MAR | APR | NOV | DEC | JAN | FEB | MAR | APR | NOV | DEC | JAN | FEB | MAR | APR | NOV | DEC | JAN | FEB | MAR | APR

him peaked for Cheltenham, but then to come back and then come back again – it takes a very good horse to do it.

'You might think he's getting easy races, but when you keep bringing him into these theatres it has to take a lot out of them. To do the three is very, very hard.'

Although any worries about the ground were ultimately dispelled, the conditions did not really play to Sprinter Sacre's strengths. Henderson said: 'If you get him on really good two-mile ground and get him jumping he's absolutely spectacular. He couldn't quite do that out of this ground. When he was Tingle Creeking and Victor Chandlering he just winged his way around. He didn't do anything wrong. He was clinical and clean. Just a very good horse.'

On the reception the horse received on his first visit to Ireland, Henderson added: 'It was special. We love coming here, we've been doing it for years. This is a nation of horse lovers and if you have a stunning horse like this you feel you owe it to everybody to come. There's no point leaving him at home.'

As for next season's campaign, Henderson said: 'It will be the same plan next year,' although Geraghty wasn't dismissive of the prospect of Sprinter Sacre staying three miles. Paddy Power quoted him as a 7-2 chance for next year's Gold Cup while offering 1-4 for him to retain his Champion Chase crown. Geraghty said: 'He's a brilliant two-miler, he's won over two and a half miles, the world is his oyster and he has all the options. We'll just enjoy today and worry about the King George nearer Christmas!' Sponsors William Hill make him a 6-4 favourite for the Kempton showpiece.

The role Sizing Europe played in this contest shouldn't be forgotten and it was as good a performance as he has put in for some time. 'The plan was to throw the kitchen sink at Sprinter Sacre and that's exactly what we did,' said trainer Henry de Bromhead. 'It's really nice to see us getting Sprinter Sacre off the bridle. He's a really special horse.' *(Justin O'Hanlon)*

"

Sprinter Sacre has an amazing presence because of his size. At Cheltenham last season I remember Channel 4 had pictures side-on as he approached the final bend. What stood out was his simply enormous stride – he seems to travel so effortlessly and yet so quickly. This horse is so exciting and so impressive to watch. He boasts a huge cruising speed and, for me, is probably the most exciting prospect in training at the moment following the retirement of one or two stars. He could be jumping's new pin-up horse.

SIMON HOLT
C4 commentator

On good ground he's spectacular, but you can't do it on this ground. It's very hard to do the three Festivals, but we wanted to come to Ireland and I'm just relieved and delighted it's worked out.

NICKY HENDERSON

From the left, Nicky Henderson, Barry Geraghty and Seven Barrows stalwart Corky Browne enjoy the Punchestown reception

RACING POST ANALYSIS: Ten from ten over fences for the brilliant Sprinter Sacre, and a job professionally done without the splendid extravagance that has characterised so many of his performances.

Naturally, the build-up was all about superlatives, and Sprinter Sacre undeniably has the profile of a truly exceptional two-mile champion. However, a colder, more clinically dispassionate analysis of this display, taken in isolation, should perhaps focus on the less spectacular aspects of his make-up.

Reading between the lines, it might not be going too far to suggest Nicky Henderson went slightly against better judgement in committing him to this final challenge of the season, a sporting decision which reflected his desire to allow the Irish public a first-hand view of the star of this season's British campaign.

As usual he travelled and jumped beautifully, but with the ground riding a bit dead, he did not exercise the utter supremacy which accompanied his wins at Cheltenham and Aintree, where the longer

Caroline Mould receives Sprinter Sacre's *Jumps Horse of the Year* for 2013 award at Sandown from Paralympian David Weir

trip did nothing to detract from his brilliance. Even Barry Geraghty used the word 'workmanlike', and if that would seem modest enough terminology for a horse of this rare calibre, it does prove that, even at the end of a period during which he has taken in the three main end-of-season Festivals, he has the all-round equipment to deal with all-comers.

This was the treat that Irish racegoers had dreamed of. No crowd ever loves horses more and for them, this day was a delight from start to finish.

Lee Mottershead was on hand to talk with them.

The horse is here but the man is not. To have the horse is a joy and a privilege. He dominates the day, his name lauded over countless pints of black stuff, but although the horse, Sprinter Sacre, is present, the man, JT McNamara is absent. Quite rightly, at the start of this tremendous Festival, we are reminded of both.

Shortly after 1pm, Nicky Henderson is escorted into the track's overflow press room. It is media briefing time, just as 6pm on Monday night was media briefing time. The trainer of Sprinter Sacre makes himself available for one interview after another, the same questions asked, the same answers given.

“

THE RACEGOERS' VIEWS

Sure it was a mind-boggling performance because the second horse ran the race of his life. It was a pleasure to be here to see the two of them. Credit to Sizing Europe because he made him go to the line, but the winner is the best I've seen since Arkle and Flyingbolt.

MICK O'TOOLE
Kildare

It was very impressive to say the least, exceptionally impressive because it was an end-of-season run and he still had the gears to pull away in the end. I came here specially to see him and I'm glad I did.

SEAMUS BROPHY
Kilkenny

He is the best we have ever seen and we are generations of Naas people coming here for years. Nicky Henderson is a legend and it was so sporting of them to allow him to run.

ANNE CURRAN
Naas

For Punchestown, all Christmases have come at once. They wanted him, they have got him and they want us to know it. Henderson, who adores this meeting and this country, is very happy to assist, but there are still four and a half hours until race time and he rather wishes there were not. ‘Let's just get it on, over and done with,’ he says. ‘Punchestown has this great idea of running the race at 5.30pm but it just drags out the agony. I'm hoping we've brought something that Ireland will enjoy watching. I'm lucky. I have the privilege of watching him every day.’

Racegoers who watch racing only in Ireland have never seen in the flesh what Henderson sees so often. Enthusiasts like Tom Keenan, an 83-year-old from Donadea, County Kildare, will get to see him, just as he once got to see Arkle. For Keenan, who has seen much in between, this is a similarly momentous experience. ‘I can't wait,’ he says, settled comfortably on a bench. ‘I've been coming to Punchestown for 64, maybe 65, years and I've never seen one better than Sprinter Sacre, not over his distance anyway.

‘Arkle was the best there's been over three miles and watching him here in those days was unreal. I've not come here as excited about a horse since then. I think he'll win by about ten lengths – and he'll do it on the bridle.’ Tom and a friend resume their conversation. All around the racecourse similar conversations are being had. In this small nugget of the racing world the talk is not of anabolic steroids, scandal and shame, but of a very special horse and what he might do a little later in the day. Expectant racegoers exchange thoughts about Sprinter Sacre and then, when they reach a trade stand by the corner of the paddock, they begin talking of something else.

From the start, the Champion Chase concerns only two horses. As one former champion enters the home straight, closely followed by an exceptional current champion, Barry Geraghty begins to look a little more energetic than we had expected. Brilliance has been blunted by the exertions of Cheltenham and Aintree but the sacred one still pulls through, not at his peak but still five and a half lengths better than the horse who before him was best. For Henderson, the agony is over.

They wait for his return, necks craned, cameras pointed. Only those of a certain vintage, only those with memories like Keenan, can remember seeing a finer creature on this Kildare soil. Then, smiles all around, glasses are charged, to absent friends and a wonderful horse, unforgettable memories on the day Sprinter came to Ireland.

3
DISASTER

PREVIOUS SPREAD: The eye of Sprinter Sacre

Fate is rarely a long-term ally and for Sprinter Sacre in particular and Nicky Henderson's stable in general, the spin of the wheel now turned against them with a vengeance. For all its conqueror's welcome, Sprinter Sacre's trip to Ireland had taken its toll and it was a leaner than usual hero who returned for his summer break in Shropshire. He also reacted poorly to a normally standard corrective operation on his palate, and after various other minor issues had delayed his progress, his planned return in the Tingle Creek was then scuppered after poor results from a tracheal wash, indicating a minor lung infection. But at least he was still in the game and had a comeback finally rescheduled for Kempton the day after Boxing Day. By then the yard was already reeling from the misfortunes of its other stars. It was a gloomy report the *Racing Post* logged after Christmas:

OPPOSITE PAGE: Sprinter Sacre and a stable mate on the Mandown grass gallops

BELOW: A mural of Sprinter Sacre winning the 2012 Tingle Creek at Sandown for the 2013 renewal. Sadly, Sprinter Sacre was unable to meet the engagement

BOBS WORTH

The Gold Cup hero trailed home 40 lengths behind Cue Card in Haydock's Betfair Chase as the 15-8 favourite last month, the first time he had finished out of the first three in 13 career

KEMPTON
Desert Orchid Chase

2013–14 **2014–15** **2015–16**

NOV | DEC | JAN | FEB | MAR | APR | NOV | DEC | JAN | FEB | MAR | APR | NOV | DEC | JAN | FEB | MAR | APR | NOV | DEC | JAN

starts. His trainer attributed the poor performance to Bobs Worth being unsuited by the track, and the gelding bids to bounce back in the Lexus Chase at Leopardstown today.

SIMONSIG

Tremendously exciting winner of the Racing Post Arkle Chase was recently ruled out for the season after failing to recover from an injury to his near-fore leg. He had been second favourite for the Queen Mother Champion Chase and his absence is a blow for racegoers who had taken him to their hearts over the past two years.

LONG RUN

Dual King George VI Chase winner and Gold Cup winner has consistently underperformed this season, beginning with a poor effort in Wetherby's Charlie Hall Chase prior to being beaten 21 lengths by Cue Card in the Betfair Chase at Haydock. He was again well beaten when unseating Sam Waley-Cohen at the final fence at Kempton on Thursday.

On the eve of Kempton Nicky Henderson said how much he was dreading the strain of putting his horse back into battle. It was a dread that proved all too accurate.

Sprinter Sacre has an appointment with heart specialist Celia Marr at Rossdales veterinary surgeons in Newmarket this morning that could determine his future after an unbeaten run of ten sensational chase victories came to a dramatic end when he was pulled up in the williamhill.com Desert Orchid Chase at Kempton yesterday.

An irregular heartbeat was diagnosed after Nicky Henderson's seven-time Grade 1 winner, sent off at 2-9 to take care of five rivals, was to general disbelief pulled up abruptly by Barry Geraghty after uncharacteristically sticky jumps at both the sixth and seventh of the 12 fences in a race won by Sire De Grugy.

OPPOSITE PAGE TOP: At Kempton Sprinter Sacre lacks his usual flair

OPPOSITE PAGE BOTTOM: Forlorn. Sprinter Sacre and Barry Geraghty after pulling up at Kempton

KEMPTON
Desert Orchid Chase

2013–14						2014–15						2015–16								
NOV	DEC	JAN	FEB	MAR	APR	NOV	DEC	JAN	FEB	MAR	APR	NOV	DEC	JAN	FEB	MAR	APR	NOV	DEC	JAN

Fears that something had gone hideously wrong were alleviated to some extent when Geraghty remained on board, trotting Sprinter Sacre up and down before a vet made a preliminary examination on the spot. It was after he had ridden the seven-year-old back to the anxious trainer for further examination near the stables area that an irregular heartbeat was found.

Geraghty said: 'He clambered over the previous fence. He felt fine during the race but all of a sudden he went from going to not going, so I pulled him up straight away. He has pulled up perfectly fine and I trotted him home just to get him back quietly. There's no concern but there was something amiss.'

Henderson, who chose to take Sprinter Sacre home to Seven Barrows for the night rather than straight to Newmarket, said: 'Both vets have listened to him, one immediately when he pulled up and the other after Barry unsaddled him. They both concur he appears to have an irregular heartbeat. One minute Barry had his tank underneath him and he was soaring along. At that last fence down the back you knew he was all right as it was Sprinter at his exuberant best. But two fences later Barry was very quick to pull him up, which was good. Barry deserves a great deal of credit for pulling him up when he did in view of what has come to light. It shows what a true horseman he is. I don't want to think what might have happened if he had continued.'

Asked how he felt, Henderson said: 'It's like someone has punched you out. You always knew it was going to come to an end [the winning run] but we're left not knowing where we are or where we are going and you feel a bit dumbstruck. The job now is to find out what happened and try to repair it.'

Sprinter Sacre was making a belated reappearance after missing Sandown's Tingle Creek Chase three weeks ago owing to an unsatisfactory tracheal wash, but Henderson is adamant that was not a factor in yesterday's performance. He said: 'The horse has been working great, jumping like he always has, and he looked unbelievable today. Everyone agreed on that.'

OPPOSITE PAGE: An anxious Nicky Henderson watches the dramatic capitulation unfold

With us in the second 4x4 was her husband Raymond, equally concerned about their public treasure. The story he told us, however, offered hope that Sprinter will return to combat as good as ever before long. Mould said: 'I'd a chaser with David Nicholson around 20 years ago called Tug Of Gold. As Alan King reminded me recently, that horse was diagnosed with the same problem as Sprinter, an irregular heartbeat. It corrected itself and a month or so later he won the Kim Muir at Cheltenham.'

As one would expect, Sprinter bossed the exercise session with the rather smaller Lough Kent, a horse with strikingly similar markings to Bindaree, Raymond Mould's 2002 Grand National winner.

As we skidded back to the yard on the saturated ground, there was time to ponder why Henderson would put himself through the added intense pressure of having the media alongside at such a critical point. So many other trainers would have carried out the test in secret. But Henderson regards Sprinter as a public horse and he deserves immense praise for his openness.

Perhaps surprisingly, hope still persisted despite all that had gone before. Indeed, towards the end of January 2014, Sprinter Sacre was even ready for some decent exercise with seemingly real prospects of making the Cheltenham Festival as if nothing had happened. David Baxter was there as a reporter and naturally heart specialist Celia Marr was the most important spectator.

Sprinter Sacre yesterday moved a step closer to a return to action, with a racecourse gallop on the cards before a return to Cheltenham to defend his BetVictor Queen Mother Champion Chase crown.

The highest-rated chaser in training yesterday completed his first piece of light work since being pulled up at Kempton last month, when a diagnosis of an irregular heartbeat threw his immediate future into doubt.

But yesterday's second set of positive results from tests on the eight-year-old's heart have given trainer Nicky Henderson increased hope his stable star will be back at Cheltenham in March for a race in which he is a best-priced evens. Earlier in the month the racing media descended on Henderson's yard at Seven Barrows to witness Sprinter Sacre canter while wired up to an electrocardiogram, and although yesterday was distinctly more low key it was no less significant. Equine heart specialist Celia Marr was again in attendance, tracking Sprinter Sacre's heart rate from a 4x4 as he was taken for a solo spin over a mile up the Faringdon Road gallop by regular partner Nico de Boinville.

Described as a 'swinging canter' by Henderson, Sprinter Sacre looked in fine form, and the trainer's assistant Patrick Harty was pleased as the pair went past, noting: 'He was striding out impressively.'

Sprinter Sacre, flanked by Simonsig, in August 2014 carries plenty of condition after six months off

Harty added: 'I've been here three and a half years and he still impresses me.' Sprinter Sacre appeared completely at ease, with his ECG readings backing that up, much to the delight of Henderson and Marr. Henderson's relaxed demeanour following a debrief told its own story, and the trainer said: 'He's come through everything we've asked today. That's the first time he's been up to those gallops since Kempton. 'He's been doing lots of cantering since Celia first came and checked him. It was fascinating watching his heart rate and all the bumps were in the right places. It's a big step forward, but we've still a long way to go.'

Marr was equally pleased by the test results, and said: 'It [his heartbeat] was completely regular. Reflecting the nature of the horse he wasn't at peak heart rate, which is a good sign of cardiac health. His heart rate was relatively low for the speed and distance he was doing, which tells you his heart is lobbing along quite easily. It was what we were hoping to see.'

Sprinter Sacre's workload will be steadily increased, and he will continue to be monitored closely when exercising, with the data sent to Marr, before another assessment next month.

An all-clear from that visit and a racecourse gallop could be the backbone of the programme for Sprinter Sacre before the Festival. Henderson said: 'He doesn't have to have a race. Racecourse gallops from our point of view are easy to control, we can go at our pace.

'With a horse like him I'm hopeful there would be racecourses that might quite like to see him, in which case I'm hoping it won't be difficult to organise. He's either got to get to Cheltenham or we're not going anywhere.'

Vet Celia Marr was a new star in the story. She had not been invented overnight. Sean Magee went to see her in Newmarket.

Drombeg Pride has a hospital appointment. The ten-year-old gelding, who failed to win in 26 outings on the Flat and over jumps and is now on the equine teaching staff at the British

Racing School in Newmarket, has been diagnosed with a heart condition that requires him to have regular, although not frequent, check-ups.

So he duly presents himself at the Diagnostic Centre at Rossdales Equine Hospital at Exning, just outside Newmarket. He doesn't know it, but Drombeg Pride is a fortunate horse, for at the hospital he is in the hands of Professor Celia Marr, whose iridescent CV includes studying at the universities of Glasgow and Pennsylvania before becoming a lecturer in the veterinary school at Cambridge, followed by spells at the Valley Equine Hospital in Lambourn and the Royal Veterinary College. Her qualifications form an alphabet soup of letters – BVMS, MVM, PhD, DEIM, DipECEIM and MRCVS.

And away from her Rossdales duties, she is editor of the *Equine Veterinary Journal*, and a driving force in the Veterinary Advisory Committee which is crucial to the

Vet Celia Marr checks the progress of this four-day old foal at the Rossdales Equine Hospital in Newmarket

process whereby the Levy Board distributes its funding to equine research.

Marr is at the top of her tree, and to the fore of late on account of her role in the diagnosis and treatment of Sprinter Sacre, whose progress after his Kempton heart scare she is continuing to monitor. But Nicky Henderson's charge is not the only jumping legend to have come under her care. In autumn 2008 she treated Denman after that great chaser had been found to have an irregular heartbeat. Indeed, she treated him so effectively that he went on to win a second Hennessy Gold Cup the following year. And when in April 2012 the highly promising Henderson-trained hurdler Spirit Son inexplicably collapsed in his box, she was extricated from a Newmarket party and, pausing only to load up the necessary hardware, headed straight for Lambourn, as Henderson memorably described in the *Racing Post*: 'Celia's arrival at about 9pm was a bit like M*A*S*H descending on us, as she and her intern swept in armed with equipment and carried out a multitude of tests and set up drips and fluids.'

Spirit Son survived a life-threatening neck injury, although his racing career was over.

Today's first patient is at the other end of the scale of eminence from Sprinter Sacre, but he still receives five-star treatment. Having listened to Drombeg Pride's heartbeat through the old technology of the trusty stethoscope, Marr wheels out the latest heart-scan equipment, a trolley-load of technical wizardry. Centrepiece of the trolley is an elaborate laptop on which is displayed, as she moves the sensor over the horse's cardiac area, images which to the layman look much like those so familiar in antenatal clinics.

Drombeg Pride's ticker is not completely pristine, and the swirl of images on the laptop feature regular little blobs of bright green, which indicate he has a minor leak from his mitral valve.

That leak in itself is no cause for alarm, but the big test will be to see how his heart performs under pressure, which means

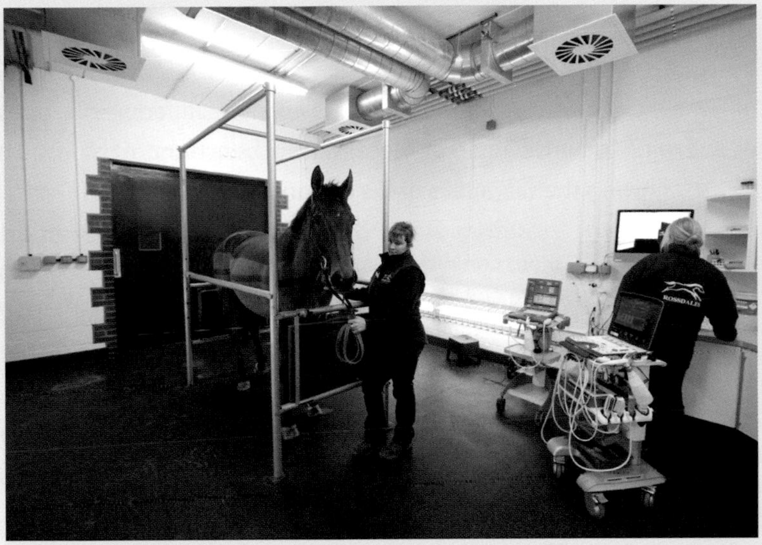

Celia Marr checks a diagnostic machine which monitors the heart of Drombeg Pride

a bout of radio-telemetric ECG in the form of a bracing canter at the British Racing School. In preparation for this next phase of his examination, Drombeg has four sensors and a small Bluetooth radio transmitter, about the size of a cigarette packet, attached securely under his girth. He is then boxed over to the BRS, and as we follow in a hospital van Professor Marr offers a brief seminar on the equine heart and her two most famous patients.

'Put simply, atrial fibrillation is a condition that causes an irregular heart rate, and steeplechasers are prone to the condition, since they tend to have a large heart in relation to their body mass,' she says. 'The bigger the heart, the greater the advantage, but heart size is by no means the sole determining factor of performance – although it is an important one – and with that advantage comes risk.

'The key difference between the cases of Sprinter Sacre and Denman is that Sprinter self-corrected and Denman required treatment, and the example of Denman shows that heart problems in horses are not related to exertion. In his case, the problem had begun during his summer holiday out at grass, and as soon as he was back cantering in the build-up to the new season, they knew immediately that he had a problem. We treated him with

Despite taking an almighty chance at one fence, Sprinter Sacre comes through his most crucial piece of work so far unscathed, while Nicky Henderson and Celia Marr look on content with his latest heart readings

when Henderson legged up Geraghty, he pranced and threatened to throw in a buck.

Henderson, possibly the only person at the racecourse not wearing an overcoat, had his nerves keeping him warm. Earlier he had walked to the edge of the paddock to inform racegoers 'he's the one at the back' to assist their identification. Owner Caroline Mould looked nervous too. She watched the work and schooling from the paddock on the big screen. She joked: 'I hope Nico [de Boinville, rider of Tanks For That] doesn't beat him.'

By then, Henderson was at the Hennessy Gold Cup start as the two horses circled. Sprinter was checked over with a heart monitor by Celia Marr, who has carried out regular tests since the fibrillating heart issue at Kempton a year ago. All previous checks had returned normal readings, as did yesterday's before and after Sprinter had covered a mile and five furlongs and jumped five fences down the back straight. Marr and Henderson observed the work from a car on the inside road.

Sprinter was pulling for his head as he tracked his stablemate. So keen was he that he took off far too early at the ditch and caught his hind legs on the fence. A brief cry of anxiety went up from the stands. That was to be his only error. From the turn into the straight, Sprinter, rated 49lb superior, steadily came clear, and there were 20 lengths between them at the

Nicky Henderson greets Sprinter Sacre in Newbury's paddock after his public schooling at the end of December 2014

winning line. Geraghty allowed him to coast the next bend and did not pull him to a stop until back at the Hennessy start. Returning to the paddock, the horse was having a good blow, a sign that there is more work to be logged before his intended reappearance in the Clarence House Chase at Ascot on 17 January. Should the ground be heavy there, plan B is Newbury's Game Spirit.

Asked about the mistake at the ditch, Geraghty was glowing, replying: 'Take that as a positive, believe me. Sprinter wanted to have a bit of a go at the fence and came out of my hands. That was an indication of how well he is. I'd have been worried if he'd put in a short stride, instead of going long like he did, because it could have indicated he wasn't as boisterous as he was.

'He was very much within himself today because the ground is testing and I didn't want to ask too much of him.'

It was the first time he had sat on Sprinter since Kempton. His next sentence was the key one: 'This was a very different experience today because this was the old Sprinter Sacre. He was full of it. You don't get that feel off many horses, if any. Fingers crossed, everything is going to be fine.'

Henderson, still without a coat, was equally bullish, saying: 'That was a massive step in the right direction. From where I was watching it looked good. Celia was happy. Barry was happy. Sprinter had a good blow, possibly more than I thought he would. I wanted to bring him here for two reasons; the timing was right before his comeback in the Clarence House, and I was keen to show him to the public. He enjoyed himself.'

The public liked what they saw and clearly appreciated what they saw. There was a round of applause and cheers as he crossed the line. 'It's wonderful the public still appreciate him,' said the trainer. *(Rodney Masters)*

The actual comeback was now scheduled for mid-January at Ascot. The racing world was on tenterhooks, and Sprinter Sacre's second place to the Frankie Dettori-bred Dodging Bullets under a tender Geraghty ride was a good enough achievement and for a few moments even gave us the feeling of 'dare to dream.'

But how far was he from the real thing? Would we ever again see 'the aeroplane' of two seasons back? Lee Mottershead set out the issue.

In defeat there was no little delight. If you were among those drawn to Ascot by his presence, or one of the many watching on television, you will have an opinion. You have yours and they have theirs, but in assessing Sprinter Sacre's comeback effort those closest to the horse were adamant. They still believe.

He was backed as if only one result was possible but on this tense afternoon no one could forecast with confidence what would happen. We knew that and so did they, which no doubt influenced the seemingly genuine satisfaction of

Sprinter Sacre enters the Ascot parade ring for his first race in nearly thirteen months

Nicky Henderson, Barry Geraghty and owner Caroline Mould despite the once untouchable Sprinter Sacre having succumbed to Dodging Bullets in the Sodexo Clarence House Chase, his first competitive outing in 386 days.

'There were no negatives at all except unfortunately he got a bit tired and got beaten,' had been the trainer's immediate reaction. A little later that had to be revised when a veterinary examination, requested by Henderson, revealed the horse had suffered a 'low-level bleed'. He was keen to play down its significance, while the rider also appeared upbeat. 'He ran a great race,' said Geraghty. 'You would have loved him to have won but he got tired. You would imagine with a run under his belt he'll improve.'

He will need to, but you would be rash to rule it out. In the minutes leading up to his return, the jumper described by some as the best since Arkle shortened to 4-6 favouritism. On the Festival's second day there will be a contest to savour. This, on the other hand, was a contest approached with some trepidation. Sprinter Sacre, dubbed by marketing folk 'the black aeroplane', had not raced since an irregular heartbeat was diagnosed after he was pulled up at Kempton two Christmases ago.

Here yesterday, following him around in the pre-parade ring, was Celia Marr watching his every move while carrying a large rucksack on her back. First thoughts were that the bag must contain an array of medical equipment, but a friend suggested otherwise. 'It's her lunch,' he said. Marr did not seem anxious and instead insisted she was 'confident'. Henderson was less bullish. 'There's nothing I can do now,' he remarked, a hint of ruefulness in his voice. 'As B Hills said to me this morning, the plane has left the runway. We can't pull out now. The plane will either crash or it won't.'

ASCOT
Clarence House Chase

2013–14 | 2014–15 | 2015–16

NOV | DEC | JAN | FEB | MAR | APR | NOV | DEC | JAN | FEB | MAR | APR | NOV | DEC | JAN | FEB | MAR | APR | NOV | DEC | JAN

Sprinter Sacre (left) fails to hold off the would-be Champion Chaser Dodging Bullets and Noel Fehily, in the 2015 Clarence House Chase as his time away from the track takes its toll

The plane did not crash but nor did it soar. Sprinter Sacre looked as gorgeous as ever, dark, sleek and athletic, but he was not match-fit and ultimately it showed. Geraghty was keen to restrain him in the early stages, when the jumping technique lacked the slickness or brio of old. Yet then a magnificent leap at the fourth-last fence took him past Dodging Bullets and, momentum created, he left behind the front-running Somersby two out. Almost immediately, however, the lead was lost to the Paul Nicholls-trained rival, who moved three lengths clear without Geraghty once touching his precious vehicle with the whip.

'He had been off the track for a year so was bound to get tired,' said Geraghty. 'He felt great and looked a winner for me everywhere through the race until we straightened up and he started to tread water.' The jockey was happy and, unless Henderson is an exceptional actor, he was similarly encouraged. 'He just got leg weary,' said the former champion trainer. 'Now we have all the time in the world. He can have a fortnight off and we can all relax a bit. We are on the right road, I'm fairly optimistic about that.

'It has been hard work. Celia always said there is the worry of whether a horse will break through the barrier. What happened to him wasn't a nice experience. In October and November he wasn't exactly blooming but things are coming together at the right time. 'There was blood in his nose when he was giving his sample but we don't think it would have affected his performance. A huge amount of horses would show a trace of blood after a race. I could have done without it, as Celia reported his heart to be 100 per cent and then this happens, but we can now take him home and do our job there.'

'I believe we're on the right track,' said Henderson. 'I can't tell you he will win the Champion Chase, but do I believe we can find a couple of lengths on Dodging Bullets? Yes, I do. If he is the target we have a realistic chance. If Sire De Grugy is ten lengths in front of Dodging Bullets we have a big task.

'We're getting there and that was another big step. He has proved it's still there.' Then, as if to emphasise the point, he added: 'And it is.'

But, crucially, is it all still there? On 11 March we find out.

On the Monday after Ascot we put the question to one of our 'Expert Juries': 'How encouraged were you by Sprinter Sacre's return to the racecourse?'

TONY SMURTHWAITE,* Racing Post *News Editor

Once the relief subsides the question becomes one of whether Sprinter Sacre can recapture his peak form. Compared to his pomp there was little to engage the senses, so it might be asking a lot to expect heroics at Cheltenham in March.

Reading the runes within Seven Barrows is not easy; whether they had the horse half-cooked, rare or well done is hard to judge and the answer would impact on analysis of his performance. Cold ratings suggest he could find the necessary small

Dodging Bullets jumps the last in front of Sprinter Sacre during the 2015 Clarence House Chase at Ascot

improvement to win the Champion Chase. But the desire where Sprinter is concerned is for a hot-blooded, passionate demolition job. It seems a stretch on this evidence.

GRAEME RODWAY, Form Expert

It was optimistic to expect Sprinter Sacre to return to his brilliant best, but it was disappointing he couldn't put his rivals away after travelling like a class act. Barry Geraghty was at pains not to give him a hard race and only went for his mount between the last two, but the response was concerning. He found nil.

It's unlikely Nicky Henderson would have left too much to work on as he needed an accurate picture of what was left in the tank. Sprinter Sacre was rated 188 at his best, yet was brushed aside by the 165-rated Dodging Bullets and looked a shadow of the horse he was at his peak.

JAMES HILL, Reporter

Let's be realistic, we didn't truly see the Sprinter Sacre of old yesterday, but he had been off the track for more than a year and it has been a tremendous effort to get him back at all. Given his recent troubles, yesterday's effort was pretty respectable and for most of the race he travelled and jumped with much of the zest and elan to which we have become accustomed.

The fact he got tired should come as no great surprise and, providing he shows no lasting ill effects, he can go to Cheltenham with a good chance of regaining his Champion Chase crown. I'd say he still deserves to be favourite.

Looking forward to Cheltenham, the main public worry may have been about Sprinter Sacre, but for a top jockey like Barry Geraghty there would surely be other concerns aplenty. Yet not many were on show when Steve Dennis spoke to him at Newbury.

Every big-name jockey has important choices to make in the run-up to Cheltenham and Barry Geraghty is no different. The cappuccino is the obvious pick, it hasn't let him down all year, no need to think too hard. The trouble comes with the sticky cake. Does he or doesn't he? The woman at the till watches him keenly, like a punter at a preview night waiting for the verdict to be handed down. He picks up the cake, justifiably thinking of the two circuits of Newbury he's just jogged, gives it a little half-regretful squeeze and then puts it down. No sticky cake.

Geraghty is an uncomplicated man, his open, cheerful face hiding little, his shoulders seemingly unbowed by any weight of expectation, his conversation unmired by angsty self-examination. The cake crisis is probably the closest he'll come all day to an internal battle and, as we've seen, it was resolved with little fuss. His wife Paula may wish to present a different angle to the argument, but from this side of a slightly coffee-stained table the man is absolutely unflappable.

'I don't feel any pressure,' he says, and the sense is that we've now moved beyond cake-gate and on into the annual

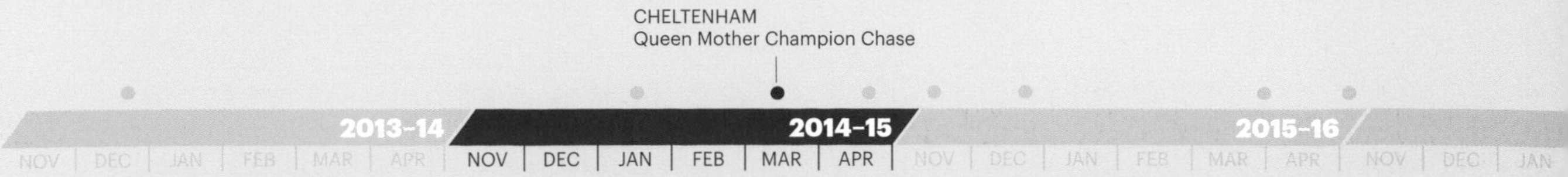

proving ground of the Cheltenham Festival, where men and horses are weighed in the balance and Geraghty has so rarely been found wanting. The Meath man has ridden more winners there than anyone but Ruby Walsh, and has won all four of the great championship contests at least twice. His book of rides this year is a proper page-turner, with enough plot twists to see him right through the week and a central character hewn wholesale from the heroic mould, and given that he hasn't drawn a blank in the Cotswolds for the last 13 seasons, it's hard to see him driving home through the dusk of Friday night without a handful of winners, if not a hatful. Yet Geraghty, conscious of the powers of hubris and aware that winners are like chickens when it comes to counting, plays as his first move the traditional Weighing-Room Defence.

'Look, I'm going in on zero, and just one winner looks very good from here,' he says. 'It's always nice to get one early, to settle any nerves, but it all depends on how the run of luck goes. The year Bobs Worth won the Albert Bartlett I'd had a wagonload of good rides on the first day, but ended up with three seconds and a third. None of them 'should' have won, I couldn't have done a whole lot better, but come Friday I'm still on zero and Bobs Worth turns into the must-win banker of the week. I was at the start thinking "all I have to do is steer this one around and it wins"; I gave the outside to no one and got the job done. It would have been a very long week without that. No, at this stage one winner looks good. I don't mind which one it might be, I'm looking forward to it all.'

It goes unspoken that Sprinter Sacre is the one he's most eagerly anticipating, because some things can be left unsaid. The great two-mile champion, rated the third-best steeple-chaser ever, has been under a cloud since his victory in the Champion Chase two seasons ago but there have recently been signs of the silver lining shining through. When Geraghty is old and grey the horse he'll be most remembered for is the tall, dark and handsome Sprinter Sacre, but there's still room to make more memories. 'I think we've got him where we want him,' he says, and perhaps it's only the imagination, but he's stirring his coffee a little more quickly now. 'I sat on him this morning [Friday] and he jumped ten fences and felt great – he's as well as we can hope to have him. I wouldn't have seen any difference today to the horse I saw two years ago. If there's a distance between what he does at home and what he'll do on the racecourse you wouldn't know, but to me he feels good. I'm very happy with him.'

Happiness was tempered with disappointment when Sprinter Sacre was runner-up on his long-awaited reappearance at Ascot in January, but Geraghty is not the type to brood over the past or let it affect the present. His confidence in the big-race favourite has not been shaken. 'His jumping was a little bit rusty, but he travelled nicely through the race before just getting a bit tired at the sharp end, which is what you

Sarwar Mohammed aboard Sprinter Sacre in February 2015, as the pair work towards Cheltenham and regaining the mantle of Champion Chaser

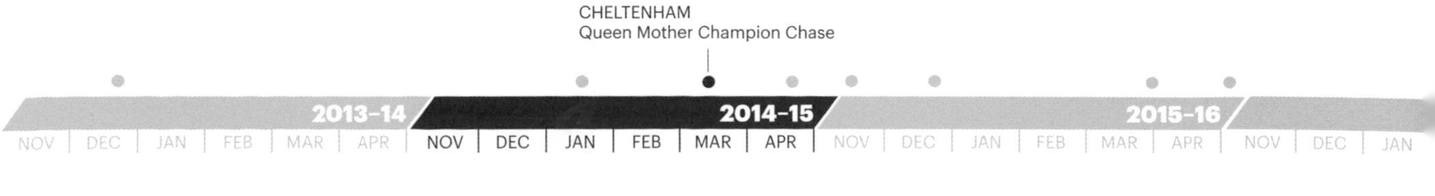

NH

Moving out of picture, Sprinter Sacre is pulled up before the last as the eventual winner of the 2015 Champion Chase, Dodging Bullets (centre), sees off the challenge from Somersby (left) and Special Tiara (right)

But he won't be abused. Everybody has worked their socks off to get him back. Nobody was pretending he was the horse he was two years ago, otherwise he would have been 3-1 on. But we've taken a massive step backwards today.'

To our surprise, and to a challenging mix of both dread and delight, Henderson began to give increasingly optimistic reports about the horse's progress. To the point where Sprinter Sacre turned out six weeks later in the Celebration Chase at Sandown. With Barry Geraghty injured the mount on Sprinter would be taken by his long-term work rider, Nico de Boinville, and together they were an honourable second to the trailblazing Irish raider Special Tiara.

RACING POST ANALYSIS: Sprinter Sacre had reportedly been pleasing his trainer in the build-up, and his regular work rider was on board for the first time in a race. It's difficult to know quite what to make of this, as he ran a solid second in a Grade 1, yet the brilliance of two seasons ago has dimmed and looks most unlikely to be rekindled. Connections were inclined to blame the watered ground, and his retirement has been deferred.

If the 'Analysis' was unsure what to make of the performance, the trainer reckoned it justified planning for another season.

Easy to say after Cheltenham, 'Thanks for the memories', but Raymond and Caroline Mould were fantastic. There was never at any stage any pressure from them. They said, 'If you want to go, go.' We needed that to give us the chance to turn him out, bring him back, have another go and if it doesn't work, call it a day.

Special Tiara, winner of the A P McCoy Celebration Chase and ridden by Noel Fehily, lands in front of Mr Mole and Tony McCoy while Sprinter Sacre and Nico de Boinville take the fence in behind at Sandown, April 2015

SANDOWN
AP McCoy Celebration Chase

2013-14 | 2014-15 | 2015-16

NOV | DEC | JAN | FEB | MAR | APR | NOV | DEC | JAN | FEB | MAR | APR | NOV | DEC | JAN | FEB | MAR | APR | NOV | DEC | JAN

4
RESURRECTION

PREVIOUS SPREAD: Nico de Boinville celebrates as the Sprinter Sacre story scales the dizziest of heights in the 2016 Queen Mother Champion Chase

HOPES OF a real revival began to gather strength soon after Sprinter Sacre returned to Seven Barrows from his holidays, and by the time of the Henderson Open Day at the end of August many claimed that he looked better than he ever had done. But such reports were still easy to compare with the 'the boy is better than ever' quotes you get from boxers' training camps and there was an unhappy prelude when Raymond Mould died in September. Yet for Henderson, bringing Sprinter Sacre and other heroes back was very much on the agenda when Steve Dennis went to see him in October.

Any trainer would be delighted to have the Gold Cup winner, Champion Chase winner and Arkle winner in his yard. Nicky Henderson is, as you'd expect, looking forward to the winter with those three big names to work with. The trouble is that Henderson has charge of the Gold Cup winner, Champion Chase winner and Arkle winner of 2013, one of whom hasn't run since, one of whom hasn't won for two seasons, and the other of whom hasn't won for almost two years. Which, naturally, both sheds light upon and casts a shadow over Henderson's prospects for 2015–16.

His chief task is one of rejuvenation, of breathing new life into his old guard, and his success in this respect will inform the yard's fortunes over the coming months. Make them the Three Musketeers again and it'll be a season to remember. Continue with the Three Stooges, however, and it may be a season to forget. That last analogy is no more than poetic licence when labelling three such superlative steeplechasers, given their mighty achievements, but it remains the case that all three have gone missing – literally, in one case – in the last 18 months. And each of the troubled triumvirate needs to trace a different path back to the summit from the base camps of convalescence, loss of form and long absence.

'All three are in good shape at the moment, touch wood,' says Henderson. 'Of course we want them back, we need them back, because those three horses have been as good as any in Britain.

In late September 2015, Sarwar Mohammed and Sprinter Sacre prepare for the season ahead in the covered ride at Seven Barrows

'One horse that good doesn't come along very often, but we had three at once. Now we have to bring them back as well as trying to find more like them. But it's one thing bringing them back to run well, quite another to get them back to their best. They aren't getting any younger, after all.'

It was understandable that Sprinter Sacre, one of the best since the peerless Arkle, failed to return to his lofty position a year after suffering from a fibrillating heart. It's impossible to say what effect his condition had on Sprinter Sacre's mental wellbeing, but in three starts last season the big black beast seemed no more than a silhouette of what he'd once been.

His magnificence was muted; second place at Ascot on his reappearance was entirely forgivable, but after that he was pulled up as he strove to regain his Champion Chase crown

CHELTENHAM
Shloer Chase

2013–14 | 2014–15 | 2015–16

NOV | DEC | JAN | FEB | MAR | APR | NOV | DEC | JAN | FEB | MAR | APR | NOV | DEC | JAN | FEB | MAR | APR | NOV | DEC | JAN

and then could never lay a glove on Special Tiara at Sandown. Calls for the nine-year-old's retirement were premature – why retire a horse who can finish second in a Grade 1? – but other, less strident mutterings along the lines of 'they never come back' may have greater resonance.

If Henderson can restore his great champion to within even hailing distance of his previous level of form, then his prospects in a muddled two-mile division would be undeniably bright, but there is perforce a 'but'. 'Sprinter looks like a bull – he looks fantastic and his demeanour is back,' said Henderson at his annual owners' day. 'He's sort of grumpy and feisty and that sort of thing was missing a bit last season. Everybody is saying he looks different to how he did this time last year, but we've got to see what happens.'

Sprinter Sacre continues his preparations for the 2015–16 season on the all-weather gallop at Seven Barrows

Little Bobs Worth needs a similar cure, after his form fell right away last season to the extent that he was barely sighted in three starts in 2014–15. Habitually lightly raced and now rising 11, there will not be too many more opportunities for the former Gold Cup winner to regain a foothold and halt his slide to a mark of 151 and falling; it would not be outrageous to consider him gone beyond recall.

Simonsig is entirely different. A series of niggling problems have conspired to keep him away from the racecourse for 878 days, have devoured the prime of his racing life, have left him almost back at square one as he approaches his official tenth birthday. His prolonged period of inactivity may make it impossible for him to recapture his novice brilliance, although previous cases indicate a degree of hope.

So if these are Henderson's trump cards, it will take considerable sleight of hand to bring one, two or perhaps all three back to the top of the pack. The genial master of Seven Barrows has worked miracles before, notably in coaxing three Waterford Crystal Champion Hurdles out of See You Then's four Waterford Crystal legs, but one horse is a project, whereas three horses – especially these three horses – are more fundamental to the health of the yard. It's the fate of the old pals' act that could shape his season.

Henderson's latest miracle, which by the season's end he himself would be calling 'The Impossible Dream', took flesh in the Shloer Chase on the Sunday of the Cheltenham Open Meeting in November. Barry Geraghty would not be in the saddle, but in opposition riding Mr Mole in his new role as A.P. McCoy's successor in the green and gold silks of J.P. McManus. So Nico de Boinville had the chance to take a full slice of the story. Sprinter's victory here may not, in form book terms, have been on a par with his glory days, but he was back. He was the hero that we had lost, and now returning into the superbly reconfigured Cheltenham paddock complex, he was found again.

It was a time to dip the pen in purple. Our writers did not disappoint.

October 2015, Sprinter Sacre with Corky Browne after his final piece of work before the Shloer Chase at Cheltenham

Save for a few unforgettable moments on March days past, this uniquely special place has seldom rejoiced with such a swell of collective happiness. It once seemed impossible, and it may still be implausible, but jump racing's second coming could yet come for a second time.

The Cheltenham faithful long since took Sprinter Sacre to their hearts and yesterday he made those hearts glad. In his pomp he was sublime, never more so than when sauntering to a massive-margin success in the Queen Mother Champion Chase of 2013. He was once described by Paddy Woods, the man who rode Arkle each morning, as the best there had been since the best there ever has been. Much, however, has happened since that comparison was made.

A heart scare kept him off the track for more than a year. When he returned for three runs last season, after one of which he bled, the nine-year-old was nothing like the awesome athlete of old. On this racecourse eight months ago he had us expecting retirement when pulled up by Barry Geraghty, but Nicky Henderson and his team, supported by owner Caroline Mould and her late husband Raymond, decided to persevere. Back at Cheltenham for his return in the Shloer Chase a once

very great animal showed that perseverance had paid off with a 14-length triumph achieved in a manner surely no one had dared to expect.

With Geraghty claimed for Mr Mole, the precious cargo was entrusted to Nico de Boinville. The race conditions favoured his mount, so much so he received 10lb from Mr Mole, but that matters much less than the fact Sprinter Sacre, for the first time in a very long time, raced like a horse who believed in himself. He jumped with elan, travelled with enthusiasm and then, when cruising into the lead at the top of the hill, delivered a wonderful sense of déjà-vu. His heart might not have been fibrillating but ours certainly were.

At the line there were 14 lengths between him and runner-up Somersby, a rival who finished second in the last two Champion Chases. They cheered him to that line and then roared him back to the winner's enclosure with a joyous reception that sent shivers down spines and, almost certainly, made the eyes of more than just one onlooker a little moist.

'He has taken us to some amazing places but probably nothing like this today,' said Henderson, whose handling of Sprinter Sacre has been masterful. 'Everybody has worked

HENDERSON'S TRIBUTE TO THE OWNER

Caroline's been brilliant all along. There's never been any pressure from her or doubt in her mind, it's always been left totally to us, even when things were going wrong – everybody felt sorry for everybody and that was as far as it went. We were allowed to do our own thing and at last he was giving us the right signals and we had good reason to be bullish, even if people were starting to say 'there's that Henderson again'.

ABOVE: Sprinter Sacre in the parade ring before his make or break seasonal reappearance in the Shloer Chase of November 2015

CHELTENHAM
Shloer Chase

2013-14 | 2014-15 | 2015-16
NOV | DEC | JAN | FEB | MAR | APR | NOV | DEC | JAN | FEB | MAR | APR | NOV | DEC | JAN | FEB | MAR | APR | NOV | DEC | JAN

4
Shloer

PREVIOUS SPREAD: There was a familiar spring in the step of Sprinter Sacre as he put in this bold jump during the Shloer Chase

ABOVE: Nico de Boinville, the new man piloting 'The Black Aeroplane', feels the reignited spark inside Sprinter Sacre

their socks off for a very long time. It has been an uphill battle. Of course there are doubters. I've been one of them at times, but this season he came back looking fantastic, completely different. I was desperately keen to get this race into him. He isn't 100 per cent but he needed that to bring him on. We are where we want to be.

'It had to happen today otherwise the doubters would have been winning the argument. The conditions of the race were in his favour, and this doesn't tell you he is where he was two and a half years ago, but we're going in the right direction. The Tingle Creek is the obvious place to go but let's see how he comes out of this first.'

The Tingle Creek could also be contested by Somersby, whose trainer Mick Channon was pleased but noted: 'When you get beaten by Sprinter Sacre you can't say anything, really.' Dan Skelton, responsible for third home Savello, agreed, saying:

'When Sprinter Sacre is in that form you're never going to beat him.'

On this occasion they came nowhere near beating him, which delighted his proud owner. 'Raymond would be very happy,' said Mould, adding: 'There obviously is a god of racing.' While she was making that divine observation, her handsome chaser was posing while fans took pictures. 'This is more a human than any horse you'll ever see,' said Henderson. 'The fact he is so appreciated by the public means an awful lot to all of us.'

That pleasure and pride was felt also by de Boinville. 'It means so much because it's all about the horse,' he said, adding: 'That was a tremendous feeling out there, probably as close to flying as you can get. I wouldn't get really carried away and go so far as to say he is back – we know it can all go wrong – but I think that's as close to being back as we're going to get.'

If it is, and especially if a few repeat performances now follow, we will not complain. Instead we will admire, applaud and be extremely thankful. *(Lee Mottershead)*

RACING POST ANALYSIS: Sprinter Sacre looked a picture in the preliminaries and resumed with the performance hoped for as he oozed class. He just wasn't near his best last season, but it was apparent from an early stage here that he was back on song and it was some sight to see him saunter clear from the fourth-last fence. He understandably got tired from the last, but his rivals were all toiling and he should be a massive player again in this division if able to maintain such form.

This was a day, these were emotions when mere form analysis was never going to be enough. To be at Cheltenham and see Sprinter looking triumphantly out over his adoring fans with those long ears cocked forward was one of the most emotional moments I have experienced in 60 years at the track.

Alastair Down caught the mood magnificently:

"

THE FUTURE ACCORDING TO DE BOINVILLE

Whether we can now go and serve it up to a horse like Un De Sceaux in the Champion Chase I don't know. So we've got to relax and enjoy this moment for the time being, after all the lows we've had with him. And then see where it leads us.

Forget doubt and sorrow, Sprinter fans are back on march to promised land.

To swipe some stirring sentiments from the old hymn:
Through the night of doubt and sorrow,
Onward goes the pilgrim band,
Singing songs of expectation,
Marching to the promised land.

On a scarce believable afternoon at Cheltenham, Sprinter Sacre took a huge step back to the future and the army of his faithful – singing songs of exultation post-race yesterday – are indeed on the march to the promised land of the Queen Mother Champion Chase.

There has been much doubt and sorrow since that day at Kempton's Christmas meeting in 2013 when Sprinter Sacre was swiftly pulled up and his long sojourn in the wilderness began. Part of the joy of Sprinter's victory yesterday was that he slew that old dragon of an adage that dolefully insists 'they never come back'. Well, Sprinter Sacre did. Not merely return from the shadows, he did so with much of the rampant imperiousness of old.

As he made his way around the parade ring he looked something he never did last year – simply magnificent. The old swagger was back and the better paddock judges were in awe of the change in him. But the test lay out of the forcing-ground of this unforgiving course which he has conquered so memorably in the past but which lies in wait like some malevolent footpad waiting to strike and expose the slightest weakness.

But the race itself proved a ludicrously pleasurable breeze and it was like welcoming back an old and valued friend who had been away for the best part of two years but had suddenly returned with all the qualities intact that had endeared them to you in the first place. This was a race you watched with a smile on your face.

Four fences out at the top of the hill, Sprinter Sacre put in a stag's leap and suddenly he was back where he belongs – tanking along in the lead in a two-mile chase at Cheltenham.

Sprinter Sacre takes off at the last with Somersby (right) chasing in vain

Quite how Nico de Boinville was feeling as they came storming down that hill is impossible to guess at. De Boinville rides Sprinter Sacre in all his work and they are almost an item. He will have been as affected by the dark days as anyone.

Sprinter Sacre was fully in charge jumping three out and putting on the Ritz again as of old. Now the voices in the stands, fuelled by the imminence of a miracle they had never really dared hope to see, began to rumble and roar the returning hero as he skipped along like a horse who'd never had a bother on him.

Over the second-last the noise built furiously and, although to my eye Sprinter Sacre looked a little leaden-footed going to the final fence, he was out on his own – just like he used to be.

Nothing was threatening to get in the same parish and he passed the line to a tumult of happy approbation 14 glorious lengths clear of the super stalwart Somersby, who was beaten just a length and a quarter in March's Champion Chase.

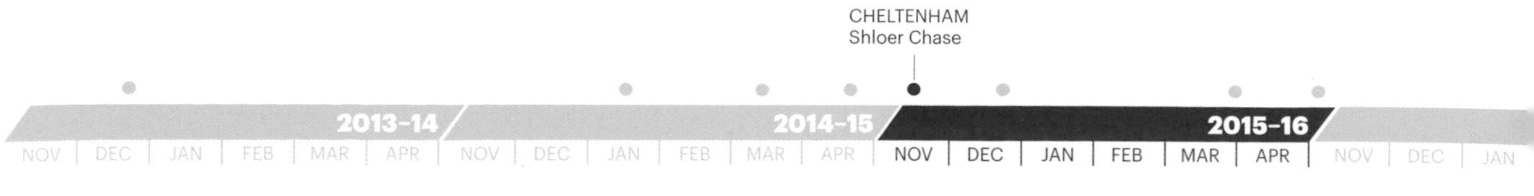

6
Shloer

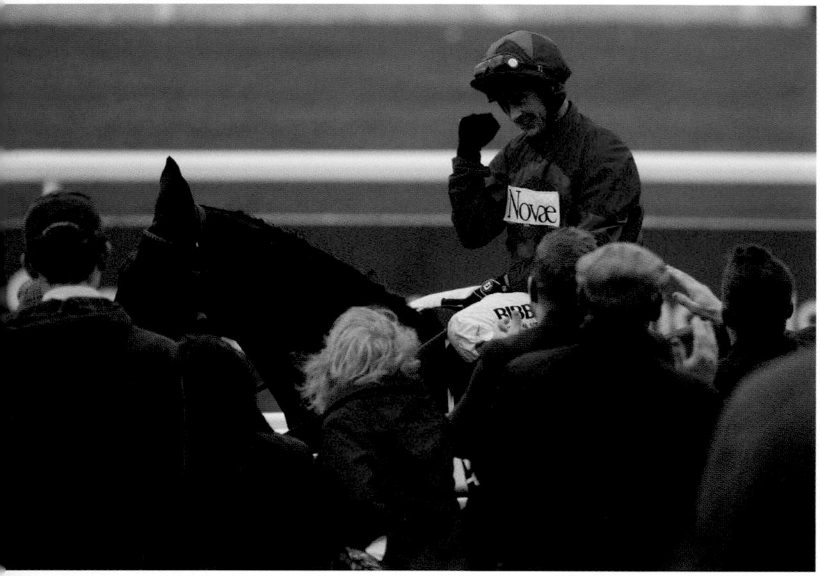

But his reception back in Cheltenham's inspired new winner's enclosure was the stuff of shivers. As we waited for the once and future king, the new upper level overlooking that precious turf quickly filled up and the steps below were rammed. We all admire those who conquer adversity, the ones with the courage to come in from the cold. And the Cheltenham crowd come to this place in the hope of some spiritual uplift and inspiration.

PREVIOUS SPREAD: Cheltenham's new grandstand plays witness to the old Sprinter Sacre as he lands over the last with his rivals toiling

ABOVE: A clenched fist in both jubilation and relief from Nico de Boinville after the Shloer Chase

As de Boinville brought Sprinter Sacre up the paddock, the assembled ranks erupted in acclamation and sheer joy that a sight many believed we would not see again had come to pass in front of our eyes, not all of which were dry. For me this was one of Nicky Henderson's finest hours and he rightly paid tribute to his team's unstinting efforts in tackling the sea of troubles that have assailed this extraordinary horse.

Many trainers would have drawn stumps after he was pulled up in last season's Champion Chase and settled for memories of the might of his prime rather than try to climb out of the pit of disappointment and attempt the impossible of putting him back on the peak. Yesterday was something of a last-chance saloon. Getting weight, Sprinter Sacre was fully entitled to win, but the manner of it sent the heart soaring.

He is not yet where he once stood but he is getting there and could very easily win the Champion Chase without being as brilliant as of old. What yesterday told us is that the fires still burn and Sprinter Sacre a few pounds off his peak could still be much the best two-miler we have. Again and again cheers and applause rang out and Henderson – proud, thrilled and moved by the moment so many have worked towards – said:

The brilliantly remastered amphitheatre of Cheltenham's winner's enclosure provided a perfect setting to welcome the returning hero

'It is very kind of the public to give him this sort of reception and all the cheering is wonderful. But I am afraid he can't hear a thing as he still has his earplugs in! So may I, on his behalf, say how grateful we all are.'

And may I, Nicky, on behalf of all those who thrill to the sight of a top-class two-miler in full flight – and perhaps this one most of all – say how grateful we are to every hand that touched the tiller that has steered Sprinter Sacre back to his harbour home in the hearts of the jumping public.

Strictly on ratings Sprinter Sacre was still some way short of the epic horse of Spring 2013. He was now a warrior, and the most popular horse in the Anglo-Irish firmament.

So the week after Cheltenham Peter Thomas went down to Lambourn.

According to the old saying, 'they never come back', and although fans of Frank Sinatra might have something to say, there's no doubting it's hard for the very best to return to the scene of past triumphs once the first blaze of their glory has been doused.

For every Elvis '68 Special there's a Spice Girls reunion tour; for every George Foreman there's a Björn Borg; for all those who bow out at the top, there are a dozen who leave the crowd wanting less; so for connections of Sprinter Sacre, last Sunday's Shloer Chase at Cheltenham was full of possibilities.

They needn't have worried. It can't be often that a horse running to within 17lb of his personal best is viewed as cause

CHELTENHAM
Shloer Chase

2013–14 | 2014–15 | 2015–16

NOV | DEC | JAN | FEB | MAR | APR | NOV | DEC | JAN | FEB | MAR | APR | NOV | DEC | JAN | FEB | MAR | APR | NOV | DEC | JAN

The ever-charismatic Sprinter Sacre is keen to show his good side when visited by the *Racing Post* in the aftermath of a remarkable Cheltenham renaissance

for national rejoicing, but when the Queen Mother Champion Chase hero brushed aside reliable yardstick Somersby and 154-rated Savello to win the 15th race of his illustrious career, the racing world fell at his feet in the same way they had when he established himself as perhaps the most talented steeplechaser of the modern era.

Nobody was fooled into thinking a Racing Post Rating of 173 was the same as his 190 demolition of Sizing Europe at Cheltenham in March 2013, but after a long spell languishing in the shadows of infirmity, here was proof that Sprinter Sacre was still a racehorse of substance – and at just nine years old he was one with time on his side.

Certainly Nico de Boinville, the new man in the saddle since the departure of Barry Geraghty, was enthused by the nature of the performance and, while not a man to get unnecessarily excited, is now allowing himself a flicker of optimism that past glories might yet be rekindled. 'It wasn't so much that he won on Sunday, more the way he went about it that impressed us all,' he says, with a hint of mild Festival fever in his voice. 'Everything went right on the day and he definitely gave me the feeling of the old Sprinter. Whether he's completely back to what he was, I'm not quite sure we'll ever get to that point, but he definitely showed glimpses of his old self in his demeanour and his swagger.'

Swagger is a commodity the old Sprinter Sacre possessed by the bucketful. As he racked up a sequence of ten straight wins over fences between 9 December 2011 at Doncaster and 23 April 2013 at Punchestown, he virtually cornered the market in the stuff; seven Grade 1 wins were achieved with more verve and elan than you could shake a stick at.

Then, however, the wheels fell off. The son of Network suffered an irregular heartbeat during the Desert Orchid Chase on 27 December 2013 and was pulled up by Geraghty after the seventh fence. Atrial fibrillation meant he sat on the sidelines for more than a year while his inferiors took advantage of his absence to mop up prizes for which he would otherwise have been a long odds-on favourite. He went from being a two-mile chaser nonpareil (he'd even won a Grade 1 over two and a half at Aintree) to being the most famous convalescent on the ward at Seven Barrows, where Nicky Henderson displayed the kind of patience only 35 years of experience can bring.

Sadly, although Sprinter Sacre's heart problem righted itself without the need for invasive treatment, the trainer's steady approach couldn't stave off a blank springtime for Raymond and Caroline Mould's superstar. He worked well at home, but only as well as any other horse, and for Henderson that wasn't enough to commit to a Champion Chase bid.

Even the Tingle Creek in December 2014 proved a bridge too soon, after an operation under general anaesthetic to re-cauterise Sprinter Sacre's palate (an issue that goes back as far as his hurdling days) 'knocked him back a little bit'. It was a period of great frustration. Leading equine cardiologist

MARR ON THE SHLOER WIN

I was astounded by the run. It was awesome and the way he stood in the winner's enclosure surveying the crowd was amazing. It's a great credit to Nicky that he's soldiered on and given the horse every chance.

“

Getting weight off those horses doesn't tell you Sprinter Sacre is where he was two and a half years ago but it's a step in the right direction. The Tingle Creek is the obvious way to go but let's see how he comes out of this race. We have been to some funny places with him but I don't think he has ever frightened me as much as he did today. We have had problems and a lot of people have tried to solve them so it's a great effort from everyone.

NICKY HENDERSON

Celia Marr continued to monitor the horse and confirmed that he seemed to be over the problem that had interrupted his career in such dramatic fashion, but when he finally made his reappearance at Ascot on 17 January this year, not only was he beaten by Dodging Bullets but he also bled from the nose. Neither trainer nor vet felt this was likely to have contributed to his defeat, but Henderson concluded he could have 'done without it', and when Sprinter Sacre was pulled up behind Dodging Bullets in the Champion Chase and then beaten by Special Tiara on the final day of the season at Sandown, the calls for his retirement not surprisingly grew louder.

Which leads us neatly to last Sunday and the race that seemed certain to define the remainder of Sprinter Sacre's career. Henderson hadn't been oblivious to the cries of his doubters and confessed to having been a doubter at times himself. He had anticipated 'some serious soul-searching' in the event of defeat, and although he declared himself upbeat beforehand, he had been upbeat before and it had not preceded unqualified success.

'Things have been pretty different this autumn,' Henderson says. 'He looks so different, completely different to last year. He came back from Juliet Minton's in Shropshire, where he's always been for his summer holidays, and he arrived looking great. I think he enjoyed my new little sand canter and spent a lot of time hacking round there, and we've had a good run with him, but I still went into Sunday as frightened as I've ever been, because it really did have to happen, otherwise the doubters would have definitely won the day.

'I think they were beginning to outnumber the believers and they were beginning to get a bit fed up with Henderson's optimism. Anyway, the conditions of the race suited him, although I was very nervous about the ground because he's a miles better horse on good going. But it was the right race for him, he was ready for a race, and it would have left us with nowhere to go if we hadn't run.

'It was nice that he was getting weight, of course, but it all depended if he was last year's model or this year's. If he was

Sprinter Sacre in all his glory

last year's, things were going to be no better, but if he was what we thought he was – something resembling two years ago – we were going to be in business.'

As far as Marr was concerned, her work with Sprinter Sacre was done. As a male horse over the age of five and an elite athlete, he had been in the group most likely to be diagnosed with atrial fibrillation, but he had self-corrected within hours of arriving at hospital the morning after the Kempton race, which means he has only a slim chance of a relapse.

'After his heart problem he went through some very detailed monitoring as he came back to training,' she explains, 'but his heart rhythm was very regular quite quickly and he got a clean bill of health. It's when you try to push on with them that things can go wrong, but Nicky has been so patient with him, and now he's back in full training it's not a problem that we'd go on and on monitoring.'

With his heart back to normal, Sprinter Sacre clearly felt like a new horse this spring, to the extent that de Boinville joined with 'back man' Tony Gilmour, vet Buffy Shirley-Beavan and the whole crew at Seven Barrows in declaring him back in possession of his rude health and his old demeanour – for better or for worse.

'A fortnight ago I walked into his box one evening and gave him a friendly slap on the neck,' recalls Henderson, 'and he just turned round and grabbed his poor lad Sarwar Mohammed by the arm – and when he wants to bite he bites. He's very feisty at the moment and as grumpy as hell in the box.

'A lot of it has to do with how he's feeling mentally,' explains de Boinville, who rode him every day at home until the demands of being a Gold Cup-winning jockey meant he handed over to Sarwar, 'and he's come back this season with bits of his old swagger back – far more so than last year. In his work we've taken it very steady with him and haven't challenged him too much, so he's enjoyed being able to get his head in front.

'We usually judge where he's at according to how he schools and he's been showing a bit of the old zip in his schooling, coming up off long strides and looking absolutely incredible. That led us to the point where we thought he was ready to run, and so he did. After all, what's a nine-year-old going to do for the rest of his life? Sit in a field when he's bred to race? If you can get him to the point where he can still pick up a few nice races, then why wouldn't you? He's still showing us that he's enjoying it, so it's worth keeping on.'

'It takes a lot of patience but you do it with any horse because that's your job, as long as the owner's patient enough and wants us to persevere,' says Henderson. 'But with a horse as good as this it's a different ball game altogether and there comes a point with a horse of his stature and popularity, who in his two golden years was unbeatable and became a hero to a lot of people, where – and I'd think the same if I was watching somebody else do it – you think how could you go on with a horse that's done you so well? I was aware that if it didn't come up trumps this time we were going to have to draw stumps.'

Sprinter Sacre may have reached last chance saloon, but the big, dark beast burst in like a gunslinger, ready to right a few wrongs, and the man on board drew comfort from knowing he was on the real deal. 'He obviously had the physical pain that left mental scars,' says de Boinville, 'and it's been a long, steady process making him believe in himself and have the confidence to do what we know he can do. But on Sunday he felt very confident. I was just strapped on, really – a passenger. The guv'nor said to me, "Whatever you do, don't disappoint him and if he wants to take you there just let him take you." Coming to the open ditch at the top of the hill he really did take me and I was just a passenger from then on.'

'It must have been very strange for Barry [Geraghty] pottering along in front on Mr Mole, to see his old mate go by him in three strides,' smiles Henderson. 'That's what he always used to do and he can kill a race that quickly. A lot of people have been saying to me wouldn't he be better over further, but when you see what he does, you can see why he's a two-miler. No stayer could take off like that.'

A carrot from his delighted handler, Nicky Henderson, is gratefully received by Sprinter Sacre

Nobody in the camp is under any illusions that the Shloer romp represented a return to the pomp of Sprinter Sacre, but there were too many positives to draw from the day to even contemplate a negative thought. Marr, for superstitious reasons, didn't go to Cheltenham – 'I love to follow horses I've helped treat but I think it's bad luck to go to the races and I prefer to watch it on the TV so I can hide!' – but for the rest of those involved it was a rollercoaster of a day, with thankfully more ups than downs.

'There were a lot of emotions, in that it was the first time there without Raymond [Mould, Caroline's husband, who died in September], who bought the horse in the first place,' says Henderson. 'It all meant so much more because of that, but now we have to sit down and decide what to do next. We rode him out this morning and he was out in the field in the afternoon, head down, just mooching about. I thought he looked very well last night, but I'd like to have a look at it all in a week's time to see how he is, but there's only one race we need to try to win and that's in March.

'We're not exactly after the money, so it's all about him, and if he says the Tingle Creek isn't a good idea, then it isn't a good idea. We don't have to go anywhere before March but we've got a sound, solid race under our belts and that's a big boost to everybody. Everyone seemed to notice the way he swaggered into the paddock and he certainly seemed to pick up on the atmosphere, which was very, very special. When he came in he had that look of eagles about him. That was him saying "I'm back".'

We might never be going to see the wonder horse of the glory days but we still faced a season no one would ever forget. Next stop was Kempton matched up by another former Champion Chaser in Sire De Grugy. Sprinter might not have dazzled us with his brilliance but he humbled us with his courage. That heart was made of wonderful stuff.

As Lee Mottershead would tell us:

A critical mistake from Sire De Grugy (left) hands the initiative, and ultimately the race, to a rejuvenated Sprinter Sacre in Kempton's Desert Orchid Chase, December 2015

Once upon a time, when his talent was such that watching eyes were rubbed in disbelief, Sprinter Sacre could saunter to success against even the strongest opposition. Different times now call for different qualities, and on an afternoon when a ghost was exorcised this great racehorse reborn passed a further crucial test.

It was two years ago to the day that what had seemed an impregnable force was halted from within. He was sensationally pulled up after the seventh fence of the williamhill.com Desert Orchid Chase, a heart issue later diagnosed. Three nervous outings last season suggested the glory days were over, but at Cheltenham in November he sent spirits soaring by storming to a wide-margin win. This time a sterner question was asked. Sprinter Sacre came up with the right answer.

He returned to Kempton for what had been his nightmare race of 2013. On that occasion Sire De Grugy had triumphed,

Two former Champion Chasers give their all, and Sprinter Sacre (right) shows a new side as he outbattles the courageous Sire De Grugy

just as he had in the Tingle Creek Chase earlier this month. Both horses have been brilliantly restored by devoted teams and yesterday they locked horns over the three fences and three furlongs of this happily buzzing track's home straight. By three-quarters of a length, and helped by a superior final leap, Sprinter Sacre and Nico de Boinville emerged victorious.

'He had to be a completely different Sprinter today,' said trainer Nicky Henderson, whose Caroline Mould-owned soon-to-be ten-year-old was trimmed for the Betway Queen Mother Champion Chase by two bookmakers but pushed out by many more, to as big as 9-2. Sire De Grugy, conversely, was widely on offer at 8-1, having been quoted at 16-1. Henderson, however, seemed delighted.

'I really do mean it when I say I've had sleepless nights about whether a horse could remember something that happened two years ago,' he said. 'There was that concern about coming back to Kempton. Would he remember the experience he had here? You would have to say there wasn't a lot wrong with his heart today because it had to be big. He had to be brave. He has the class, but sometimes you have to tough it out as well. I thought the other horse was getting the better of things, but he came back and fought.

'We could get him to the Queen Mother without a race as there are other things after Cheltenham. He's just as good fresh as very fit, so I'd be maybe leaning towards not running again before Cheltenham. He hasn't got back to his very best yet, but we're getting there. Everything is working, that's the great thing. There are no holes in him now but it won't ever get any easier, as we love him to bits.'

The Moore and Preston families love Sire De Grugy just as much. The more positive tactics employed here once again could conceivably upset the rhythm of Un De Sceaux, still hot Champion Chase favourite despite falling at Leopardstown. What is not in doubt is the white-faced star who took the Cheltenham crown of Sprinter Sacre is back, as evidenced by his clear beating of Vibrato Valtat and Somersby in third and fourth.

'I've no excuses, although we'd have preferred the ground to have been softer,' said trainer Gary Moore. 'I was hoping he might get back up, but all respect to Sprinter Sacre and Nicky Henderson. At least it bodes well for the Clarence House at Ascot, and maybe Sprinter Sacre won't be there.'

More visibly downbeat was rider Jamie Moore. 'I'm gutted,' he said. 'It's as simple as that. The race went well and although the mistake at the last didn't help we were beaten fair and square.'

The horse who beat him was 'a bit below' his Shloer Chase form according to de Boinville, but there was an explanation.

'He had to show a lot of character,' he said. 'That track was sharp enough for him as he couldn't use his stride and jumping, but up against an in-form Sire De Grugy it was one heck of a performance.

'It's very special to bring him back to somewhere close to where he used to be. I don't think we can judge him on a track like Kempton, I think we should judge him around Cheltenham.'

When he takes on Un De Sceaux, Sire De Grugy and hopefully reigning champion Dodging Bullets as well, that judgement day at Cheltenham should be something to savour.

RACING POST ANALYSIS: A fascinating affair. There was a strong gallop set and two top-class chasers locked horns in the home straight.

Sprinter Sacre looks out towards the statue of Desert Orchid, after whom this race was named

Sprinter Sacre made it 2-2 for the campaign with a brave success to rid the demons of pulling up with an irregular heartbeat in this race two seasons back. He was back to near his old self when scoring decisively at Cheltenham in November and was entitled to beat old rival Sire De Grugy on that form, but the brilliant 9yo had to really fight for this prize. Indeed, he briefly looked held after two out, but found extra and crucially produced the better leap at the last. This did look plenty sharp enough for him, something his master trainer reasoned afterwards, and showed a different side to him in the finish as he has often sauntered to success, so he deserves plenty of credit. With Un De Sceaux falling on his return at Leopardstown earlier in the day, the Champion Chase has a more open look to it at present, and the general 9-2 on offer looks perfectly fair for his bid to land it for a third time. Heading straight there – which is most likely the plan – makes plenty of sense.

Alastair Down had written plenty on both triumph and disaster. Now he was reporting on a mighty scrap – and loving it.

Two top-class chasers with a place close to the heart of many a jumps fan fought a tooth-and-claw tussle in yesterday's Desert Orchid Chase with Sprinter Sacre just edging out Sire De Grugy in the sort of confrontation you'd walk many a mile in tight boots to see.

First and second were in the air together with Vibrato Valtat both four out and three from home, but going down to the second-last it was the big two head to head and the crowd, stuffed with partisan supporters of both horses, went to town on the encouragement front as they roared on their particular favourite. Jamie Moore tore into Sire De Grugy on the run to the final fence and for a moment it looked as if the seventh member of the Moore family was getting the better of the battle.

Sprinter Sacre needed a brilliant jump at the last, and that is exactly what Nico de Boinville conjured from him and it may even have contributed to Sire De Grugy making a mistake

“

I got the feeling two miles around here is sharp enough for Sprinter Sacre. He couldn't sweep past them like he can on a stiffer track. He has the ability to gallop relentlessly at a good pace and this track probably just caught him out a little. I thought the other horse was getting the best of things but he came back and fought. There was that concern about coming back to Kempton and would he remember the experience he had here. You would have to say his heart was in it today. It's another step forward, a different step this time. He is just as good fresh as he is very fit so I would be leaning not to run again before Cheltenham.

NICKY HENDERSON

which, at that stage, took the race from deuce to advantage Lambourn. But my God how Sire De Grugy fought his corner and Sprinter Sacre had to dig proper deep to hold his rallying opponent by three-quarters of a length.

Two-mile chasers are often about sheer brilliance and yesterday's protagonists have given us some magnificent moments. But on this occasion it came down to guts and grind and you could not separate them on that front – both gave their all. There is certainly a case to be made that the last fence cost Sire De Grugy victory, but typically Gary Moore was making nothing of it. And on ground not as soft as his horse would like and round a course that wouldn't play to his strengths, Sire De Grugy ran a blinder.

The important thing about this win was that it was Sprinter Sacre's first back-to-back victory since the days of his overwhelming pre-eminence. It tells us a great deal about Sprinter Sacre's reinvention because there is no such thing as two flashes in the pan. Nico de Boinville nutshelled it when saying: 'He's very special and it's great to have him somewhere near where he was.'

That's the nub of it – somewhere near. The team at Seven Barrows have indeed worked wonders with Sprinter Sacre and it's a pleasure to have him back punching at the top level.

But nobody is pretending he is the force of old and Nicky Henderson is clearly going to mind him in the run-up to the Festival – almost certainly going straight there as there is loads of evidence Sprinter Sacre is best fresh.

Henderson harked back to 2013 when he sent his star to Cheltenham, Aintree and then Punchestown, which was three runs from 13 March to 23 April. It was all done for the best reasons – to give the Irish a sight of him – but as Henderson said: 'That third race was one too many. He might have made things look easy, but it was anything but.'

The last two days have marked an upturn in Henderson's fortunes after a December that has served up slim pickings. A double on Boxing Day and a second win in a row for

From left to right, David Minton, Caroline Mould, Nico de Boinville and Nicky Henderson pose for photographs after winning the 2015 Desert Orchid Chase

Sprinter Sacre hopefully mark a return to form. Surprisingly, Henderson said he had been having genuinely sleepless nights over whether Sprinter Sacre would have any memories of this day two years ago when his heart issues suddenly turned the apparently invincible into the mortal.

He joked he can't remember things that happened two days ago and happily Sprinter Sacre proved cut from similar cloth. There is no profession more superstitious than the training one.

Henderson also made the valid point that Kempton's two miles is plenty sharp enough for Sprinter Sacre now and that he 'couldn't sweep round them like he used to on a stiffer track'.

There would be no more runs before the Festival but there was still plenty to learn from trainer and jockey. Alastair Down went to see them.

KEMPTON
Desert Orchid Chase

2013–14 | 2014–15 | 2015–16

NOV | DEC | JAN | FEB | MAR | APR | NOV | DEC | JAN | FEB | MAR | APR | NOV | DEC | JAN | FEB | MAR | APR | NOV | DEC | JAN

This time he will be in the spotlight but he has already absorbed the need to treat triumph and disaster with equal deference, which may explain why he seems encased in a vacuum of mild detachment. He is courteous yet guarded with words, willing yet simultaneously hesitant, happy to converse until he decides the line of questioning will unravel no further. What comes across with particular resonance is his raging ambition. You could knock him over a thousand times before he would even consider taking a count.

His raw desire emerges from a vignette he relates about his long association with Sprinter Sacre. The horse was allocated to him from the moment he arrived at Henderson's yard in 2009, a few months after he left Newcastle University following one term. He was still a teenager, yet the impact he made on Henderson's backroom staff was such that he became integral to the stable's daily rhythms when a more seasoned hand might have been summoned.

De Boinville schooled and worked Sprinter Sacre alongside big-name jockeys aboard big-name horses, yet two years down the line, when Geraghty was unavailable for the dark bay's chasing debut at Doncaster, Henderson called on David Bass. He could hardly have turned to de Boinville, who had yet to ride his first jumps winner under rules. Nevertheless, de Boinville's fires burned so fiercely that he had to swallow hard.

'David [Bass] is a great mate,' he says, 'but on the day he rode Sprinter at Doncaster I went and schooled some point-to-pointers. It was tough to deal with; you had to suck it up. I was very lucky to be on him in the mornings but that wasn't what my aims or intentions were. My end goal was to ride them in the afternoons.'

He now has his wish, particularly in respect of Sprinter Sacre, whom he will ride in the Betway Queen Mother Champion Chase. He is uniquely well placed to assess a horse who has had well-publicised problems for the previous two seasons. After winning the Cheltenham Gold Cup, de Boinville gave up his daily vigil with Sprinter Sacre as he pursued his race-riding ambitions, but when they were reunited on Henderson's gallops in the autumn he instantly noticed the difference.

'We've seen a complete turnaround,' he says. 'We still don't know whether it was his confidence. I think his heart problem had something to do with it and there were various other things, although we could never categorically pinpoint what it was. But now he's happy and he looks in great order. He's absolutely flying at the moment.'

Sprinter Sacre is among a number of prominent horses de Boinville will ride at Cheltenham, although Coneygree's injury means he will sit out the Gold Cup. In sharp contrast to 12 months ago, the jockey will walk through the weighing-room doors with an entirely different mindset this time. He is no longer a wannabe desperate for a break. He will be auditioning for one of the sport's most coveted jobs in the public glare of the four-day Festival. It is exactly as this intensely focused young man would wish it. Whether he can kick down a door

January 2016, Sprinter Sacre (centre) walks back across frozen turf to Seven Barrows after exercise. The overnight temperature had dropped to -10°C

Sarwar Mohammed and Sprinter Sacre before his tilt at the Champion Chase of 2016

that is halfway open will probably make it a career-defining week. Nobody is more aware of that than the man himself.

DE BOINVILLE ON THE RACE: I imagine Un De Sceaux is going to do what he has always done. Hopefully I can keep tabs on him and at some point really test him. I won't be waiting until the last before launching my challenge, although with Sprinter you'd have to do it when he wants to do it. He definitely tells you.

That's the one thing the guv'nor always says: 'Whatever you do, don't disappoint him.' He's very settled now through the early part of a race but there comes a time when the others start to tire, or their jumping comes under pressure and they start to make mistakes. That's when he comes into his own. He has surprised me by the way he has come back. And I was very surprised by the way he battled it out in the Desert Orchid, when he beat Sire De Grugy. I didn't think that was him really, but he showed a lot of guts that day.

So to the Cheltenham showdown. Of course the facts made it possible but memories of the heart failure at Kempton two seasons back and of that sad canter back into seeming retirement only a year ago suggested otherwise. Great was the rejoicing.

RACING POST ANALYSIS: An intriguing Champion Chase, featuring last year's brilliant Arkle hero up against the last three winners of this event, all of whom had a certain amount to prove. The pace was sound and the first three home dominated from the off.

Sprinter Sacre, whose jumping was by no means fault-free, moved smoothly to the front on the home turn and was soon in a commanding lead, although he was tiring up the hill. This was an astonishing display by the brilliant 2013 winner, whose career has stuttered due to a heart problem and for whom retirement has been mooted more than once. For him to get back to this level at the age of ten is a tribute to the skill of his trainer, as well as to the horse's courage.

This was 'The Impossible Dream' come true. All of us there felt the privilege of watching history being made, a sentiment shared by journalists too. Let Lee Mottershead tell the tale.

There are great horses and great races, but exceptionally rare are the life-enhancing moments that impart such a sense of joy and euphoria that you know immediately the memory will stay with you forever. We savoured such a moment yesterday when witnessing the unlikely and unforgettable resurrection of the incomparable Sprinter Sacre.

This course is synonymous with performances that have shaped our racing lives, none more so than the Gold Cups of Arkle, Dawn Run and Desert Orchid. By regaining the Queen

Mother Champion Chase against all the odds, three years on from the triumph that led some to hail him the finest horse in half a century, Sprinter Sacre delivered a display every bit as extraordinary.

On this day 12 months ago he seemed finished. The superstar chaser with the matinee idol looks had come back from the heart scare that derailed his career, but on the track he once ruled, the Festival faithful saw with sorry eyes a pale shadow of the athlete they once lauded. He cantered up the home straight after being pulled up by Barry Geraghty. Had his retirement been announced we would not have been surprised, nor would we have complained. Indeed, we would have thought it for the best.

Yet many of the thousands here at Cheltenham will never have seen better than this comeback to top all comebacks, nor will they have been able to salute a finer piece of training than that executed by Nicky Henderson and his Seven Barrows team. Two victories from two starts this season sowed the seeds, while recent home reports had been bullish, but still we could do no more than dare to dream.

Caroline Mould's ten-year-old returned to the Betway-backed Champion Chase as 5-1 second favourite. The thrilling 4-6 favourite Un De Sceaux, trained by the unstoppable Willie Mullins, lay in wait. Yet when one followed the other during the pre-race parade it was Sprinter Sacre, black, gleaming and impossibly beautiful, who stood out. So he did in the race.

Sensationally, Un De Sceaux found not only one better at the end but also one faster at the start. It was not until after the final ditch he got past Special Tiara, but his own time in front was brief.

Running away from the third-last fence, at a stage when Un De Sceaux appeared to be cruising, Sprinter Sacre ranged alongside under Nico de Boinville before galloping further and further clear. You could almost see the look of astonishment on Un De Sceaux's face.

Special Tiara (right) takes on Un De Sceaux who is unable to carry out his usually dominant tactics. Sprinter Sacre and Nico de Boinville are poised right behind

They cheered Sprinter Sacre all the way up Cheltenham's home straight, and although he tired in the closing stages the final margin of supremacy over Un De Sceaux was considerable. 'We are in a little bit of wonderland here,' said Henderson, teary-eyed. 'This is the most rewarding moment I can remember. My biggest moment of doubt was coming off the top of the hill as Ruby [Walsh] was tanking on Un De Sceaux. That's the first time in the last month I've thought this won't happen. Then, ten strides later, I knew it was going to happen. We were optimistic in the past. Today we had to be pretty bullish. In his first Champion Chase he was so dominant but he must have been good today.'

De Boinville could testify to that. 'This has been playing on my mind for a long time,' he said. 'Ruby got away slightly at the top of the hill, but once you go down the hill Sprinter seems to get into another gear. All I could think when we went alongside

PREVIOUS SPREAD: 'The Impossible Dream' becomes reality as Sprinter Sacre carries Nico de Boinville over the final fence in the Queen Mother Champion Chase 2016

OPPOSITE PAGE: Ruby Walsh on Un De Sceaux (left) congratulates a euphoric Nico de Boinville

Un De Sceaux was, "Let's see what you've got Ruby." We got to his girth and then he just took off. It was phenomenal.'

For the 26-year-old rider, victorious on Coneygree in last season's Gold Cup, this was also deeply emotional, as on Valentine's Day he lost his 59-year-old mother Shaunagh to cancer. 'Obviously it has been difficult,' he said, adding: 'She might be looking down on us.'

If she was, she would surely have been filled with pride. Mould, whose own husband, Raymond, died last year, owns a magnificent racehorse, but she was just one of tens of thousands willing him home, many of whom then sprinted to see Sprinter Sacre return to that famous winner's enclosure. The noise they made will top anything heard here in a very long time.

'I know he wanted to do this,' said Henderson. 'He is a treasure – of course he is. How can a horse know he is good-looking, but I know he does. He is an exceptional racehorse as well. He has the charisma that makes this so special. He has built his own atmosphere today. We say thank you to everybody who has supported us and him, but, in a funny way, I think this was Sprinter's own way of saying thanks.'

This was indeed a day to say thanks and to be thankful. A very wonderful day indeed.

Training Sprinter Sacre had put Nicky Henderson through the mincer. But as he looked back at this second Champion Chase three years after the first, and just twelve months since 'Sprinter' had been pulled up in disarray, he really had something to savour.

It all looked so easy when he won here three years ago. I promised he would go to Punchestown – and I wanted to go because you know how much the Irish appreciate horses – but I've never forgiven myself for doing it. We slotted Aintree in the middle and I wondered whether we had got to the bottom of him. We underestimated how much winning on the bridle took out of him. We had a lot of soul-searching to do but we've

CHELTENHAM
Queen Mother Champion Chase

2013–14 2014–15 2015–16

NOV | DEC | JAN | FEB | MAR | APR | NOV | DEC | JAN | FEB | MAR | APR | NOV | DEC | JAN | FEB | MAR | APR | NOV | DEC | JAN

Novæ

come up with the right conclusion. When things weren't going quite so well we had a lot of support from everybody. We were never put under any pressure. There wasn't a baying for his retirement. That was much appreciated.

For two years people have been very kindly writing what I've said while probably knowing I've had my fingers, toes and everything else crossed. We had to be positive and to try to think we were getting there, otherwise the game would have been over. However, in the last few weeks there were stories of great gallops taking place – and they were. The last time he schooled two weeks ago he was just like he used to be. This time our positive vibes were pretty honest. The horse in the paddock on this day last year compared to the horse you saw today are two different animals.

You also shouldn't underestimate how important Nico de Boinville has been in the horse's whole life. In the early days he was riding him, schooling him and getting him ready for Barry Geraghty. Nico deserves every accolade because he has done this horse really proud. A lot of people do like this horse, which helped us get through it when things weren't so good. I thank everybody who has been part of his resurrection – because that's what it has been.

RACING POST RATINGS: Although rated a stone below that level, Sprinter Sacre (176) earned the best winning figure for the race since the 190 he posted in 2013. Having twice recorded an RPR of 173 this season, there was a good chance better ground would tease a higher figure from him and, given that he lost momentum at the last and understandably tied up a bit close home, he was value for a bit further than the winning margin. *(Steve Mason)*

Alastair Down had expressed how Sprinter Sacre's Cheltenham comeback had been extraordinary but this was something extra. The champion had been lost but was now found again. It could not happen. But it had.

“

Sprinter Sacre has been a very special horse. For those two golden years he was unbeatable. I said he couldn't come back to his best, but maybe he has. He had to be as good as he ever was to do that. We had to be positive in that he was improving but there has been a complete difference in the horse this year. He came in looking great in the summer and when you see him in the paddock today compared to last year, they were two different animals.

NICKY HENDERSON

OPPOSITE PAGE: The rapturous celebrations begin

Well done Nicky Henderson!!!
TOTEPOOL
15:39

Everyone wanted to prove that they were there

Amid scenes unparalleled even at this old spell-weaver of a racecourse we witnessed the return of the king yesterday with Sprinter Sacre overcoming his sea of troubles to reclaim his rightful place at the very pinnacle of jump racing. This was a victory, in magnificent defiance of the odds, which rendered the old adage 'too good to be true' forever redundant.

And, my God, how the Festival faithful wallowed in the sheer wonder of it, draining the cup of joy in a vast collective 60,000-strong gulp. The potion brewed by Sprinter Sacre was heady stuff indeed and how happy Cheltenham felt to be elevated into a state of total intoxication. At one stage Sprinter Sacre was rated the finest two-mile chaser ever seen but that mean old judge the head told the heart that a return to the Olympian heights was surely the stuff of dreams. And one of

A reaction like no other, Nico de Boinville with arms aloft greets the Cheltenham faithful

the joys was the way in which Nico de Boinville and Sprinter Sacre – 'a terrible show-off' in the words of this trainer – put on a performance that was pure theatre.

Yet coming down the hill the outcome still hung ominously in the balance and de Boinville was scrubbing his old ally along as they ran to the last, where the 2013 champion chaser was far from fluent. But what happened next was like the sun coming out. Suddenly Sprinter Sacre surged into the lead and we all immediately sensed the race was Seven Barrows-bound and one of Cheltenham's most momentous hours was before us.

Part of the beauty was that the heaving enclosures, watching the scarce-credible coming to life, had the time to revel in the spectacle. There was none of that looking back for challengers or the fear that something could come and destroy the dream.

CHELTENHAM
Queen Mother Champion Chase

2013-14 | 2014-15 | 2015-16

NOV | DEC | JAN | FEB | MAR | APR | NOV | DEC | JAN | FEB | MAR | APR | NOV | DEC | JAN | FEB | MAR | APR | NOV | DEC | JAN

This was quite simply Nicky Henderson's finest hour, surpassing all his other many achievements. Tear-stained but in seventh heaven he handled the moment with brilliance and modesty but admitted no other win had given him such pleasure. It has been a team job at Henderson's and many a hand has lain on the tiller that has steered Sprinter Sacre back to harvest home. How he and Corky Browne, a platoon of vets, de Boinville and Sprinter's much put upon lad Sarwar Mohammed have wrought this miracle only God and they will know. Poor Sarwar is regarded as nothing more than a tasty snack by Sprinter, who regularly takes a lump or two out of his arm. But you would not begrudge this horse of the ages a whole arm plus a second one for pudding if he fancied it.

Yesterday Cheltenham delivered one of those enriching experiences that draw us all here year on astounding year. Sprinter Sacre must be made of sterling stuff as he has been through plenty and had the temperament, tenacity and toughness to tread a hard road. He has proved to be one for the long haul. And while the horse is always the hero, on this occasion the trainer is the man of the hour.

For yesterday, for the improbable happy madness of an indelible afternoon, we should simply say thanks to Nicky Henderson for working something close to a miracle. Sprinter Sacre is champion chaser once more. An equine eighth wonder of the world.

Whose horse is he anyway? When something becomes as much of a national treasure as Sprinter Sacre, it seems to belong to everyone. Not just to Caroline Mould, the actual owner, or Nicky Henderson, or Nico de Boinville, but to the whole adoring public outside. Yet the closest person to him on a daily basis is all too often forgotten. It was good to put it right after Cheltenham.

SARWAR MOHAMMED, 40, GROOM OF SPRINTER SACRE:
We had some difficult times with the horse, as everybody knows, and people were wondering if he is going to be able to

produce a performance that was anywhere near his best, but seeing him in his preparation I was happy that he was fine, in very good form and ready to go. I'd have to say I was a little nervous before the race. I came to the yard more than seven years ago – having been a work-rider at the Hyderabad Race Club – and I've looked after Sprinter Sacre and ridden him since he came here, so I'm very attached to him.

Once the tapes went up I was able to enjoy it because he was always travelling and jumping so well.

Sarwar Mohammed at Sprinter Sacre's head after the 2016 Champion Chase

The closer they got to the finish, the more the nerves grew again, but when he reached the second-last fence I started to believe he could win, because I knew he was fit and well and able to run to the line. After that there was a lot of excitement as he pulled clear of the others, and it was a big moment for everybody in the yard. It was great to hear all the noise coming from the grandstand and the crowd was brilliant.

They all seemed very happy for Sprinter and were delighted to see him winning such a big race after so many problems, but it didn't surprise me to see him running so well because I knew the boss had done a great job in getting him back to top

One last sight of their Champion, Sprinter Sacre seals his triumphs with a lap of honour around Cheltenham's parade ring

form, and I was 100 per cent confident he could do himself justice. He was fine after the race and has been fine ever since, which makes the win even better for us, and personally, now we know he can perform as well as ever, I'd love to see him run again and give everybody some more great moments.

Sarwar's wish was to be granted on the last day of the season in Sandown's Celebration Chase, and the performance was to match the title. In the paddock 'Sprinter' looked better than ever, and out on the track he was close to awesome. We celebrated with him.

This was a day when champions were crowned, all of them human, but the greatest heroes of horseracing, particularly jump racing, are the horses and on the season's final afternoon, to much rejoicing, we again saluted the sport's four-legged renaissance wonder, the incomparable Sprinter Sacre.

There has been no better advertisement for racing, nor indeed for the talents of trainer Nicky Henderson, than the animal whose breathtaking beauty is matched by his brilliance, which in his latest tour de force was again gloriously evident.

At Cheltenham in March he provided a moment to treasure when regaining his Queen Mother Champion Chase crown three years after he first won the race and 12 months after he was pulled up in the same contest, immediately causing many of us to think his racing days were over.

How marvellous it has been to be wrong.

There have been four chances to see Sprinter Sacre over the last six months and he has not once let us down. That was certainly the case here at Sandown, where he followed his Cheltenham triumph with a sublime encore performance that left Henderson and jockey Nico de Boinville daring to suggest Caroline Mould's ten-year-old was now tantalisingly close to the form that once made him unbeatable in the hands of Barry Geraghty. 'He felt fantastic,' said de Boinville. 'That was somewhere near to what Barry used to tell me he was like.

We went a good gallop but I still had to keep taking a pull. He was very good.'

Very good indeed. The betting suggested Un De Sceaux would defeat Sprinter Sacre at Cheltenham and the final odds here almost swung in the Irish raider's favour once again. However, as in the Champion Chase, the confirmed front-runner was hassled up front, this time by Sire De Grugy. The harassment impacted on his jumping, most notably at the Pond Fence, which Paul Townend's mount got badly wrong.

Sprinter Sacre was not foot-perfect there himself, but it mattered not one jot. He powered clear, eventually thumping Un De Sceaux by 15 lengths with the fast-finishing Dodging Bullets a length back in third, one place in front of Sire De Grugy. 'He just took off – I didn't realise how far clear we were,' said de Boinville. Henderson did and he delighted in what he saw, just as he deservedly enjoyed the special round of applause afforded him by racegoers.

'It's all a bit unreal really,' said Henderson. 'We never dreamt this could happen, which is why Cheltenham was called the impossible dream. Why did we have to do this today? Why did we have to put ourselves through it again? I was looking for every possible excuse not to run him, but there weren't any. His work was good, he looked amazing and his schooling was brilliant.

'He isn't exactly what he was in the old days but he would be pretty hard to beat now. We'll be bumping into Douvan next and that will be another ball game, so I suspect we have to keep going.

'I'm dying to stop and let him open supermarkets, but why pack it in now? This is what makes National Hunt racing. He enjoys racing and racing enjoys him.'

Un De Sceaux never really looked like he was enjoying the Sandown experience. 'He just wasn't sharp enough,' said trainer Willie Mullins, adding: 'He lost a shoe but I don't think that made any difference.' To his credit, Un De Sceaux battled bravely for second, while Dodging Bullets worked hard up the Sandown hill, looking for all the world like a horse who needs further.

So, too, might Sire De Grugy, whose trainer Gary Moore said: 'We are a soft-ground horse, Sprinter Sacre is a good-ground horse. Maybe time is catching up with him.'

We thought time had caught up with Sprinter Sacre but we have seen these past few months he is a champion not just of the past, but also the present. 'I wasn't nervous,' said de Boinville before collecting another trophy. 'You just have to enjoy being able to ride such a fantastic, magnificent horse.' In this spectacular season, watching that fantastic, magnificent horse has been a rare and wonderful pleasure. *(Lee Mottershead)*

RACING POST ANALYSIS: Sprinter Sacre, fresh off a remarkable Champion Chase win, had apparently been in cracking form at home and, with the leaders taking each other on from a long way out, and big market rival Un De Sceaux making a race-ending blunder three out, he was left to waltz clear. He'll be 11 next year and will presumably have Douvan to cope with, but whatever he achieves in future this season has been one to remember for a horse who'd been written off.

As ever Sprinter Sacre summered at his second home in Shropshire. Whatever the future, it was time to end this tribute with a final talk with those closest to him, and a glorious country pilgrimage one golden day in June.

"

For two awful years it just wasn't there. It has been a long, slow process but this season Sprinter Sacre came in looking in really good shape. He isn't exactly what he was in the old days but he would be pretty hard to beat now. We'll be bumping into Douvan next, and that will be another ball game, so I suspect we have to keep going. I'm dying to stop and let him open supermarkets but why pack it in now?

NICKY HENDERSON

HUMPHREY
BUTLER
LTD
Stobart
BUTLER
LTD
4
et365.com

OUT TO GRASS

BROUGH SCOTT

HE STANDS on the brow with the old oak behind him and the distant hills ringing the horizon. Sprinter Sacre is back at his summer home in Shropshire and no resting hero ever wore his greatness more proudly.

Out in the field many fine horses slip back to muddy ordinariness and – to take the line from Philip Larkin's poem At Grass – 'stand anonymous again'. But that won't ever happen with Sprinter Sacre – neither his physique nor his fame will allow it. Even after a full two months' holiday out in the paddocks of Juliet and David Minton's Mill House Stud, just south of the little old town of Much Wenlock, he looks anything but the big common slob some old chasers turn to in the summer. He looks big and bold and ready. And you only have to say his name. He is Sprinter Sacre.

Mind you, he wasn't when he first came here way back in February 2008. As David Minton loves to relate, he was just a big unbroken two-year-old, part of the legendary 20-horse 'job lot' that 'Minty' and vet Buffy Shirley-Beavan were despatched at a day's notice to buy on behalf of the late Raymond Mould. 'The truth is that he was just another good-looking young horse,' says Juliet Minton as she looks across at the now famous arched neck and long pricked ears of our hero. 'There were a mix of two-, three- and four-year-olds and I remember they were all nice horses.'

In the last 20 years Juliet and David have transformed what was once her family's farm into a thriving breeding and boarding operation. It would have been she who gave Sprinter Sacre his first lessons in long reins and she who during the summer still supervises the two bowls of nuts he gets night and morning. Caroline Mould is Sprinter Sacre's devoted and official owner, but a great horse like him tends to also belong to a lot of people, from Sarwar Mohammed back in the stable to the public in the stands.

PREVIOUS SPREAD: Final hurrah. Nico de Boinville drives Sprinter Sacre up the Sandown hill to a victory in the Celebration Chase

Sprinter Sacre, a picture of greatness

The Mintons' share of that sense of ownership is as warm as it is longstanding.

'We feel very involved with him – there's been a big team of very committed people around him along the way,' says David Minton, who can never suppress a rubicund smile when he thinks of the 15 other winners besides Sprinter who came from what proved to be the bargain price of €300,000 for that 2008 consignment.

Out in the field Sprinter Sacre has an acolyte: Jenkins is a big handsome four-year-old whose career is where his senior's was six seasons ago. Like Sprinter, he has had just two impressive runs in bumpers, winning brilliantly at Newbury and then being an unlucky loser at Punchestown. Like Sprinter Sacre back then, he could be anything. But what a road he will have to travel to even be mentioned in the same breath as the horse beside him.

Once again the memories cloud in: Newbury, Cheltenham, Aintree, Sandown; that almost royal visit to Ireland, the shattering, world-fall-in moment at Kempton; Barry Geraghty in the scarlet silks locked on to the awesome 'Black Aeroplane' of Sprinter's absolute zenith; Nico de Boinville stepping up from morning duty to the glory of last season's impossible dream. It's warm summer in Shropshire but the head fills with the commentator's calls of the winter game. That's what happens when you get an audience with greatness – and you are even allowed to rub his neck and scratch his back.

Such privileges are granted only in holiday time. The stories of what Sprinter can do in his box to the unwary, and even to the long-suffering Sarwar Mohammed, are exceeded only by how much Henderson's first great star See You Then would chew his trainer and anyone else within biting range. In their boxes they are dictators; the field is more of a democracy. See You Then was surprisingly subservient out at grass and if Sprinter Sacre could never be that, he is a big friendly presence. In sporting terms there is something very special in this intimacy. It's as if it was quite normal to walk into the pub and have a pint and a chat with Wayne Rooney or Andy Murray without any previous acquaintance.

Early next month Sprinter Sacre will travel back to Seven Barrows for the start of another season, one more summer under his belt, one more step along the extraordinary story that started in deepest France on the foaling day of 23 April 2006. It is diverting to think that if he were a human athlete Sprinter, like Kauto Star, would still talk with a French accent and that the most famous Frenchman to visit Much Wenlock had come way back in 1890. That's when Baron Pierre de Coubertin stayed with Dr William Penny Brookes and watched the Doctor's brainchild, the already 40-year-old Much Wenlock Olympian Games. It was from this idea that the good Baron took the idea into the holding of the first Modern Olympiad at Athens in 1896.

De Coubertin is most famous for saying 'it's not the winning, it's the taking part'. Well what he really said was 'ce n'est pas le triomphe, mais le combat', but then he was French. Such warm sentiments are no longer enough for most Olympians and for all their obvious affection for their charges, it is continuing success that drives everyone from Juliet Minton long-reining her beginners to Nicky Henderson belying his pensioner status as he relishes the challenge fresh talent gives him.

This drive certainly applies to Phil and Mel Rowley, who run a high-achieving point-to-point yard at Poplar Cottage a dozen miles down the road towards Bridgnorth and who took on the second stage of Sprinter's education along with three others who made the job lot journey up from France.

For six weeks in that first year the young hopeful would have been progressed as far as cantering upsides and even popping over a few poles. With that in his head he did not return until a full winter of work as a three-year-old that would have included regular groundwork sessions under Grand Prix standard Mel Rowley to develop the core muscles which are now accepted as a vital base for an athlete's frame, whether it be carried on two legs or on four. 'He was very straightforward,' says Phil. 'I don't remember anything special about him except that he was very workmanlike and that he did everything with a smile on his face.'

During this time came one of those 'Sliding Doors moments', on which, in racing as much as in all life, so many fates are hung. Raymond and Caroline Mould had come down to look at their as yet unnamed horses and to decide in whose colours they would run and to which of Nigel Twiston-Davies and Nicky Henderson they would go. The four horses, two bays and two browns, were all much of a promising muchness, and an actual process of selection does not appear to have undergone much detailed debate beyond Raymond saying something like: 'Why don't I take the bay ones and you have the brown ones?'

Caroline Mould now looks back with sometimes tearful pride on what that exchange with her late husband has brought in its wake. 'I can't pretend to have thought Sprinter was anything extra back then,' she says, 'and I can't begin to describe the pleasure and the pain. The people involved have been marvellous but it has all become so overwhelming that sometimes it seems as if he is everybody's horse.'

Sprinter Sacre (left) with Seven Barrows stable-mate, Jenkins, at Juliet and David Minton's Mill House Stud near Much Wenlock in Shropshire

Such are the consequences of greatness yet, as ever in racing, even a horse as unique as Sprinter Sacre has to be parked in the waiting bay while the daily treadmill keeps turning. Presently it turns painfully for Barry Geraghty as he nurses a broken arm and ruefully looks back at 'the great times we had together'. He talks of that extraordinary track record-breaking day at Newbury, the triumphs of Cheltenham, the horror of Kempton but above all the power and elasticity of his jumping stride. 'He is some horse,' says Geraghty, in the ultimate of understatements.

Nico de Boinville has nothing but happiness to add as he pushes on with 19 winners already notched for the new season. 'It was such a phenomenal year,' he says, 'and all the better for being fairly unexpected and at Sandown he really felt better than ever. I feel so lucky to have ridden a legend.' The thrill of association is felt across the board albeit, in the case of Buffy Shirley-Beavan and Celia Marr, having both been linked to super heroes previously, Shirley-Beavan with Kauto Star and Marr with Denman.

Sometime in October, Sprinter Sacre will have a full MOT but neither practitioner expects there to be any problems. 'At ten years old he is pushing 40 in human terms,' says Marr, 'but it's other tissues rather than the heart that begin to weaken.' To which Shirley-Beaven adds that last season the old problems with his back and stomach ulcers were better handled than ever, not least with Henderson's introduction of the new water treadmill to aid the ongoing work of Tony Gilmour on the Sprinter Sacre spine.

Gilmour's 40 years go back to chiropractor days when treatment of horses had to be mixed with urgent manipulation of world champion showjumper David Broome's back on the kitchen floor. 'The great thing about a good yard,' he says, 'is that everyone talks to each other. They are all trying for the best outcome.'

That's certainly the case at Seven Barrows, to which Sarwar Mohammed will shortly return from his holidays in Hyderabad, and where Corky Browne continues to be a daily inspiration to all, and where Nicky Henderson is still restlessly buoyed not just by past achievements but by the hopes up ahead.

'We call last season The Impossible Dream,' he says, 'and he has become such a public horse that we are just the curators now. So of course we will draw stumps if there are any signs of deterioration or if Douvan slays him in the Tingle Creek. But horses have a way of speaking to you – he certainly does, and if he tells us he is ready for it, the public deserve to see him take his chance.'

So the mind closes on that horse on the brow of the hill and to all those racetrack images that flare in the memory. But win or lose, run or retire, he has already done what very few can ever do. He has given us something that we can hold down the years. We can say that we saw Sprinter Sacre.

RESULTS

(AT CLOSE OF 2015–16 SEASON)

SPRINTER SACRE (FR)
10-y-o (23Apr06 b/br g)
Network (GER) — Fatima III (FR) (Bayolidaan (FR))

TRAINER Nicky Henderson
OWNER Mrs Caroline Mould
BREEDER Christophe Masle

JUMPS PLACINGS 11/2113/11111/11111/P/2P2/1111-

LIFETIME RECORD	STARTS	WINS	2NDS	3RDS	WINNINGS	EARNINGS	BEST TS	BEST RPR	OR†
NHF	2	2	0	0	£9,758	£9,758	108	131	—
Hurdle	4	2	1	1	£8,864	£21,054	149	151	149
Chase	18	14	2	0	£1,052,860	£1,106,072	170	190	175
Rules Races	24	18	3	1	£1,071,481	£1,136,884	—	—	—

DATE	RACE CONDITIONS	WGT	RACE OUTCOME	JOCKEY	OR	TS	RPR
23Apr16	San 15.5Gd C1ChG1 71K	11-7	1/6 (15L Un De Sceaux 11-7) 11/10F	Nico de Boinville	175	170	176
16Mar16	Chl 16Gd C1ChG1 199K	11-10	1/10 (3½L Un De Sceaux 11-10) 5/1	Nico de Boinville	170	159	176
27Dec15	Kem 16GS C1ChG2 45K	11-10	1/5 (¾L Sire De Grugy 11-10) 8/11F	Nico de Boinville	173	120	171
15Nov15	Chl 16GS C1ChG2 42K	11-0	1/6 (14L Somersby 11-0) 15/8F	Nico de Boinville	167	149	173
25Apr15	San 15.5Gd C1ChG1 71K	11-7	2/7 (6L Special Tiara 11-7) 4/1	Nico de Boinville	167	149	164
11Mar15	Chl 16Gd C1ChG1 199K	11-10	PU/9 (Dodging Bullets 11-10) 9/4F	Barry Geraghty	179	—	—
17Jan15	Asc 17Sft C1ChG1 70K	11-7	2/5 (3L Dodging Bullets 11-7) 4/6F	Barry Geraghty	—	156	170
27Dec13	Kem 16Sft C1ChG2 45K	11-10	PU/6 (Sire De Grugy 11-10) 2/9F	Barry Geraghty	188	—	—
23Apr13	Pun 16Sft ChG1 100K	11-12	1/5 (5½L Sizing Europe 11-12) 1/9F	Barry Geraghty	188	115	179
05Apr13	Ain 20Gd C1ChG1 113K	11-10	1/6 (4½L Cue Card 11-10) 1/3F	Barry Geraghty	188	120	190
13Mar13	Chl 16GS C1ChG1 208K	11-10	1/7 (19L Sizing Europe 11-10) 1/4F	Barry Geraghty	179	153	190
26Jan13	Chl 16.5Hy C1ChG1 39K	11-7	1/7 (14L Mad Moose 11-7) 1/5F	Barry Geraghty	179	107	178
08Dec12	San 15.5Sft C1ChG1 68K	11-7	1/7 (15L Kumbeshwar 11-7) 4/11F	Barry Geraghty	169	159	178
14Apr12	Ain 16Gd C1NvChG1 56K	11-4	1/4 (13L Toubab 11-4) 1/7F	Barry Geraghty	169	140	170
13Mar12	Chl 16Gd C1ChG1 74K	11-7	1/6 (7L Cue Card 11-7) 8/11F	Barry Geraghty	169	165	176
17Feb12	Nby 16.5GS C1ChG2 17K	11-5	1/6 (6L French Opera 11-10) 2/5F	Barry Geraghty	161	160	171
27Dec11	Kem 16Gd C1NvChG2 13K	11-6	1/3 (16L Peddlers Cross 11-8) 11/10	Barry Geraghty	—	124	162
09Dec11	Don 16.5Gd C4NvCh 3K	10-10	1/6 (24L Lightening Rod 11-1) 2/9F	David Bass	—	146	154
15Mar11	Chl 16.5Gd C1NvHG1 57K	11-7	3/15 (5¼L Al Ferof 11-7) 11/1	A P McCoy	145	149	151
19Feb11	Asc 15.5Sft C2NvH 6K	11-7	1/8 (7L Polisky 10-7) 30/100F	Barry Geraghty	137	97	138
05Feb11	Ffo 16GS C4NvH 2K	11-3	1/8 (10L Sorcillera 10-10) 2/9F	Barry Geraghty	—	104	126
19Nov10	Asc 19.5GS C3NvH 5K	10-12	2/12 (1¾L Frascati Park 10-12) 6/5F	Barry Geraghty	—	128	132
17Apr10	Ayr 16Gd C4NHF 4K	11-4	1/12 (4L Yes Tom 11-2) 13/8F	Barry Geraghty	—	88	131
20Feb10	Asc 15.5GS C3NHF 5K	10-9	1/14 (nse King Of The Night 11-8) 8/11F	Barry Geraghty	—	108	108

INDEX

Page numbers in *italics* refer to illustrations.